PETRODVORETS

Vadim ZNAMENOV

PETRODVORETS
Palaces
and Parks

A GUIDE

RADUGA PUBLISHERS
MOSCOW

В. Знаменов

ПЕТРОДВОРЕЦ, ПУТЕВОДИТЕЛЬ

На английском языке

Редакция литературы по спорту и туризму

Translated from the Russian by *Kathleen Cook*
Editor of the Russian text *Y. Brodsky*
Editor of the English text *A. Kafyrov*
Designed by *V. Miroshnichenko*
Art editor *A. Tomchinskaya*
Maps by *L. Cheltsova*
Layout by *S. Sizova*
Photos by *B. Manushin*

3 $\dfrac{1905040100\text{-}368}{031(05)\text{-}86}$ 058-86

ISBN5-05-000689-9

CONTENTS

PÉTRODVORETS

The marble obelisk by the railings of the Upper Gardens in Petrodvorets has the numbers 26 and 29 engraved upon it. The first indicates versts (the old Russian measure of distance) and the second—kilometres. This was the distance from the Obvodny Canal, the old limit of St Petersburg, to Peterhof, the former country residence of the Russian Emperors and now the world-famous park and palace museum ensemble of 18th- and 19th- century Russian art in the town of Petrodvorets.

In May 1703 at the mouth of the River Neva Peter the Great founded the city of St Petersburg which became Russia's new capital in 1712. To defend the town from attack by sea construction began in 1703 of a fortress, subsequently called Kronstadt, on the island of Kotlin which guarded the entrance to the eastern end of the Gulf of Finland. Peter himself supervised the building of the fortress. The way to the fortress from St Petersburg was by sea, but in bad weather you had to travel along the southern shore of the Gulf, where a small house was built for the tsar to rest.

To the east of this in 1714 construction began of the Upper Chambers (the future Great Palace). It was not fitting for the tsar to stay, albeit for a short while, in a cottage. So work began simultaneously on the construction of a small palace called Monplaisir. Drawings and notes on documents show that the overall plan and the detailed design of some architectural elements belong to Peter the Great, a man with a remarkably wide range of knowledge.

The first general plan of Peterhof was drawn up in 1716 by the architect Johann Friedrich Braunstein. It shows that by this year the layout of the central and eastern sections of the Lower Park was completed for the most part. In 1720 construction began on the Château de Marly, thus determining not only the western limit of the park, but also its architectural centre from which three avenues fan out across the park from west to east. A year later the Hermitage Pavilion was built on the seashore symmetrical with Monplaisir. Together with the avenue from the Upper Chambers to Monplaisir and the Marine Canal, the avenue to the Hermitage Pavilion formed another trident running from the terrace to the sea. This completed the main network of avenues.

The Lower Park was set out like a typical formal French garden. As in Versailles it was originally conceived as a park with fountains. In selecting this site for Peterhof, Peter took into account the abundant supply of water that could be used to feed the fountains. The tsar entrusted the planning of the hydraulic system for the fountains to Vassily Tuvolkov, aged twenty-three, who had studied hydraulic engineering in Holland and France. Under his supervision in the summer of 1721 the sluice and ducts were installed along which the water first flowed to Peterhof on 9 August, 1721. Construction of the fountains and improvement of the hydraulic system continued up to the middle of the 19th century.

The formal opening of Peterhof took place on 15 August, 1723. By then some of the fountains were already working, the Upper Chambers, the Monplaisir Palace and the Château de Marly had been built, and the Hermitage Pavilion nearly completed. With the death of Peter the Great in 1725, followed by that of his wife Catherine I in 1727 building in Peterhof ceased. The court moved back to Moscow, and the Imperial residence fell into neglect. The buildings became dilapidated, the paths overgrown, and only when Peter's niece Anne ascended the throne in 1730 did Peterhof come to life again: new fountains were built and those begun during Peter's lifetime were completed.

The real flowering of Peterhof is associated with Peter's

8   daughter Elizabeth who ruled from 1741 to 1761. Between the mid-forties and the mid-fifties the architect Bartolomeo Rastrelli turned the Upper Chambers into the sumptuous Great Palace, built the Catherine Wing of Monplaisir and designed some new fountains.

In 1762 as a result of a palace coup the Russian throne went to Catherine II. The new Empress's interests and ideals were in keeping with the Classical style then prevalent in Russia. In 1779 she commissioned the architect Giacomo Quarenghi to begin construction of "New Peterhof" to the south-west of the Upper Gardens. Quarenghi designed the English Park and built the English Palace, a fine specimen of Classical architecture.

Subsequent masters brought "good" and "bad" times in the history of Peterhof. Some monarchs forgot about it and left it to decay, while others remembered it and new fountains, sculptures and palaces appeared in its grounds.

The October Socialist Revolution changed the life and significance of Peterhof radically. Its parks, palaces and art treasures were made the property of the whole Russian people. All the possessions of the Imperial house of the Romanovs were handed over to the state by decree of the Soviet Government.

A commissar was dispatched to Peterhof to organise the preservation of the palaces and parks, and a special commission listed the works of art. More than ten palaces and pavilions were turned into museums. They illustrated the development of Russian and West-European art from the 18th to early 20th centuries. In May 1918 the Great Palace opened its doors to the first visitors, a group of Petrograd workers.

The 1941 season was due to open on 22 June, but on that very day the Nazis invaded the Soviet Union. In the first few weeks several trainloads of museum exhibits were removed from Peterhof to safety far away from the enemy. Some exhibits were moved to Leningrad. The marble sculptures were buried in the Lower Park and the bronze was hidden in an old drainage tunnel on the slope of the terrace below the Great Palace. But a great deal could not be removed or hidden in time. On 23 September the Nazis broke into Peterhof.

The same day they set fire to the Great Palace, burnt the Catherine Palace of Monplaisir and devastated the Monplaisir Palace itself. The Hermitage Pavilion was also sacked and looted.

The sculptural groups of the Great Cascade that had not been removed in time, Samson, the Neva, the Volkhov and the Tritons, were either stolen or destroyed. The English Palace was destroyed down to its very foundations, and the Château de Marly blown up.

The Lower Park was a mass of dug-outs and trenches, its avenues strewn with piles of felled trees. An anti-tank ditch ran across the Upper Gardens, and the invaders completely destroyed the hydraulic system.

This barbaric occupation came to an end on 19 January, 1944, when Soviet troops liberated Peterhof. It looked as if it would never rise from the ashes again. At the Nuremberg Trials the destruction of Peterhof was described as a crime against humanity.

Restoration work began almost immediately after liberation. Another year of war lay ahead, but the architects were already drawing up designs for reconstruction and restorers were studying valuable fragments of architectural details. The fountains and hydraulic system were repaired, and the statues dug up and restored to their former places. The formal opening of the Lower Park took place on 17 June, 1945, and the following year the first Petrodvorets fountains began to play once more.

The vast funds allocated by the state for restoration work made it possible to raise the buildings of the Lower Park from the ruins in a relatively short time. In 1952 the Hermitage Pavilion was reopened, to be followed by the resurrected Monplaisir Palace. In 1964, on the day marking the 250th anniversary of Peterhof, the first few rooms of the Great Palace were reopened to the public.

Today Petrodvorets has 144 fountains, 3 cascades, and six

10   museums. Restoration work still continues, however. Its aim is not only to heal the wounds inflicted by the war, but also to restore the gardens and parks to the form in which they were originally planned.

Today the newly-resurrected palace with its parks has acquired a new significance: it is not only a treasure-house of history and art, but also a monument to the dedicated labour of the architects, painters and craftsmen who have raised up out of the ruins and ashes the splendid works fashioned by the hands of our ancestors.

Upper
Gardens

Let us begin our visit to Petrodvorets with the Upper Gardens that adjoin the Great Palace to the south. The park covers an area of 15 hectares between the facade of the Great Palace and the main road to Leningrad. The green lawns and fountains of the broad parterre flank the central axis symmetrically and enable one already at the main entrance to survey the palace in all its splendour. The whole layout of the Upper Gardens is centred on the palace. It plays the role of a magnificent courtyard or cour d'honneur for the Great Palace.

In the first quarter of the 18th century the Upper Gardens was known as the kitchen-garden. It grew vegetables, dill, parsley and other herbs, and various medicinal plants. The fountain bowls erected at the suggestion of Jean-Baptiste Alexandre Le Blond were not just reservoirs for the fountain system, but were also used as fish ponds. Thus, the Upper Gardens performed domestic tasks, first and foremost.

By the second quarter of the 18th century, however, the vegetables and fish ponds had been replaced by avenues of finely clipped trees, trellis summer-houses and richly ornamented fountains that gave the small area the appearance of a formal garden. The wrought-iron railings erected in 1755-1759 and designed by Rastrelli that enclose the park on three sides became an important element in its appearance.

For more than two centuries the trees and shrubs in the park were tended and replaced. Apart from the traditional lime trees and fruit trees, there were horse-chestnuts and maples, jasmine and rose bushes, and even sweet-scented grasses. Little care was taken to preserve the old layout of the Upper Gardens in the 19th century. The trees grew unchecked until they obscured the facade of the palace, the clear lines of the symmetrical French garden were lost, and when shrubs were planted in the central parterre, the splendid vista was lost completely. Not until 1926-1929 was the first attempt made to restore this unique park to what it looked like in the first half of the 18th century.

During the occupation of Peterhof the Nazis did a great deal of damage to the Upper Gardens: they felled many trees, destroyed the fountains and looted the statues that had not been hidden. One of the columns at the main gate was blown up. When the enemy were driven out it was decided to restore the park to what it looked like during the period of its greatest flowering, i.e., the first half of the 18th century. This was the first attempt at the restoration of a park ensemble of this kind.

Work began in 1956. First the old trees were removed. They appeared to be strong and healthy, but on closer inspection it was discovered that each tree was full of bullets and pieces of shells and mines. They could not have stood for much longer. In their place twenty-year-old limes were planted, as well as fruit trees, thuya, box hedges and hawthorn bushes. The drainage and fountain systems were repaired and the sculptures of the fountains were restored. By 1968 the restoration of the Upper Gardens was for the most part completed and it was reopened to the public.

We invite you to start your excursion at the main gate adorned with Corinthian columns. Our first stop will be a composition of five fountains that has survived to the present day.

MEZHEUMNY FOUNTAIN

Immediately behind the Corinthian columns of the main gate in a large open area sprinkled with sand is a round basin with four

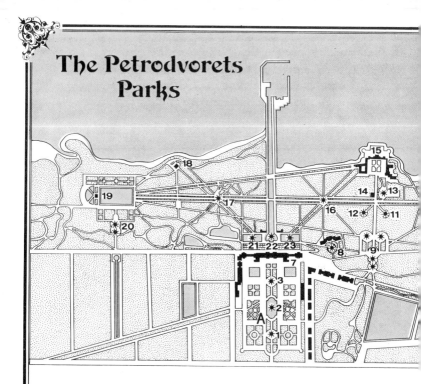

The Petrodvorets Parks

A. UPPER GARDENS
1. Mezheumny Fountain
2. Neptune Fountain
3. Oak Fountain
B. ALEXANDRIA PARK
4. Capella
5. Cottage Palace

6. Farm Palace
C. LOWER PARK
7. Great Palace
8. Triton Fountains
9. Chess Hill Cascade and
    Roman Fountains
10. Pyramid Fountain

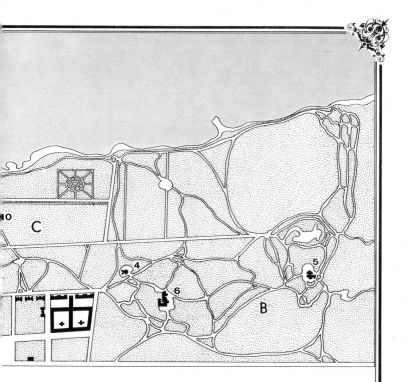

16 dolphins and a dragon in the middle. Jets of water shoot out of their open jaws.

This fountain has the somewhat strange name of Mezheumny, which used to mean "indeterminate". The name reflects the many changes that have been made in the sculptural ornament of the fountain. In 1738 a sculptural composition by Rastrelli showing Perseus defending Andromeda from the dragon was set up in the middle of the fountain that had been built the year before. It was later replaced by the dragon and four dolphins, which at the beginning of the 19th century gave way to the sculpture of a fish that stayed there for about half a century.

When the fountain was restored, it was decided to use the second version of its sculptural ornament, known from a drawing in an 18th-century album. The dolphins and dragon were cast in bronze in 1958 from models made by the sculptor Alexei Gurzhy.

NEPTUNE FOUNTAIN AND APOLLO CASCADE

The compositional centre of the Upper Gardens is a large, rectangular fountain with semicircles along its short sides. The hole for it was dug in 1721, when the first stage of the Peterhof fountain system was completed. The actual fountain did not appear until thirteen years later, however, when Rastrelli suggested casting a sculptural group called Neptune's Chariot from a model made by him at Peter the Great's request in 1723.

Thus, in 1734 a large composition of seventeen gilded lead figures representing Neptune in a chariot drawn by four sea-horses was installed in the Upper Gardens. Naiads and sirens frisked around him. The group was crowned by a ball of gilded bronze raised high on a jet behind Neptune's back. At the same time a small three-tiered cascade was set up on the south side of the fountain, with a gilded lead figure with a brazier cast back in 1721. The figure was called Winter. But the lead sculpture began to crack and by the end of the century looked rather dilapidated.

Main entrance to Upper Gardens

View of Apollo Cascade and Neptune Fountain

Great Palace from Upper Gardens. Oak Fountain

Neptune Fountain

In 1799 a new composition was installed in the central fountain of the Upper Gardens. The events which led up to this are as follows. In 1782 the heir to the Russian throne Prince Paul (the future Emperor Paul I) was travelling in Europe and in the town of Nuremberg purchased a Neptune fountain group made in the middle of the 17th century. When Paul acceded to the throne and it was decided to renew the sculptures of the Peterhof parks this purchase was remembered. In the summer of 1799 the new Neptune fountain sculptural composition was installed in the Upper Gardens.

On a high pedestal stands the figure of Neptune holding a trident pointed downwards in his right hand and wearing a crown. The two nymphs below seated on barrels symbolise the rivers Pegnitz and Rednitz that flow through the lands of Nuremberg. Next to them are twin figures of riders on sea-horses and four cupids on dolphins and sea monsters. On the pedestal are coats-of-arms, mascarons and cupids blowing trumpets. When the fountain was installed it was decided not to renew the gilt that had come off most of the figures, but to paint the old gilded figures of dolphins that remained from the Rastrelli fountain the colour of bronze.

In place of the figure of Winter that had also survived from the old fountain, and in keeping with the tastes of the new age, the Belvedere Apollo, so popular in the Classical period, was set up, a copy of the original by the Greek sculptor Leochares.

During their occupation the Nazis destroyed the statue of Apollo, dismantled the sculpture of the Neptune fountain and dispatched it to Germany. It was found after the war, with the exception of a few elements and one of the riders, and returned to Petrodvorets. The sculptor Vladimir Tatarovich reproduced the lost details, and the fountain was restored.

OAK FOUNTAIN

This circular fountain lies equidistant from the Neptune and Mezheumny fountains to the south of them. Its name has long since

26 lost its original meaning and testifies only to the original ornament of the fountain.

Construction on it began in 1734. The following year an oak tree, three tritons and six dolphins made of lead from a model by Rastrelli were cast. The oak was soon dismantled, however, to be set up in the Lower Park more than fifty years later.

In the second half of the 18th century a carved and gilded Horn of Plenty was placed in the centre of the bowl. It was repaired and replaced several times, before disappearing finally. Only the dolphins continued to send up high jets of water. In 1929 a marble figure of Cupid putting on a tragic mask was set up in the centre of the fountain. It was made in 1809 by the Italian sculptor De Rossi.

During the occupation the Cupid was saved, but the dolphins were destroyed by the fascists. After the war the Cupid was returned to its former place. The six figures of dolphins lying on mounds of tufa were recast in bronze.

SQUARE PONDS FOUNTAINS

In 1719 large square ponds designed by Le Blond were dug on the right and left of Peter the Great's Upper Chambers, which were to serve as reservoirs for the fountain system of the Lower Park. In 1737 the sculptural groups of Diana with Nymphs and Persephone and Alpheius were installed on circular, granite-faced pedestals in the centre of each pond. Six gilded lead dolphins spouting jets were placed around each group. In the second half of the 18th century the groups fell into disrepair and were replaced by vertical jets of water.

During the war the Nazis destroyed the dolphins and fountains of the Square Ponds. In 1956 the dolphins were restored. In the centre of the west pond a marble statue of the Italian Venus was erected, a 19th-century copy of the original by the Italian sculptor Antonio Canova, and the east pond was adorned with a marble figure of young Apollo, a copy from the Greek original.

Great
Palace

The structural centre of the Upper Gardens and the Lower Park is the Great Palace. The axis of the parterre in the south and the straight line of the Marine Canal in the north are both perpendicular to its centre. The palace stands on the edge of a sixteen-metre high terrace, adorned with gold statues, the crystal jets of the Great Cascade and the terrace fountains. The gleaming gold, the exquisite architecture and the splashing of the fountains create a most impressive sight.

The palace was not like this originally, however. Nor was its role as the architectural centre of a splendid ensemble determined right from the start. Peter's original plans were very modest. In 1714, at the same time as the construction of the Marine Canal, the grotto and the cascade, work began on some modest Upper Chambers with a heated (winter) and an unheated (summer) section. Judging from the documents, the author of the first plan for the chambers was Peter the Great himself. The building was carried out by Johann Braunstein. It proceeded "with haste" and by 1716 the small building with its rather ordinary architecture was ready.

Neither the appearance of the chambers nor their dimensions were in keeping with the role of the building as the centre of the splendid park ensemble which had already been conceived by that time.

Also in 1716 the new chief architect Jean-Baptiste Le Blond presented Peter with a design for rebuilding and extending the building. His design was not approved in full. A certain amount of rebuilding was carried out, however.

In 1721 Niccolo Michetti, who succeeded Le Blond as chief architect, presented his design for extending the Upper Chambers, which not only envisaged increasing the dimensions of the palace, but also, most important, disregarded the original compact plan of the chambers, the breadth of which was restricted by the Great Cascade.

He added a long, single-storey gallery on either side of the existing building ending with two-storeyed side pavilions containing living quarters. These two side pavilions were in line with the Chalice Fountains in the parterre and the flowerbeds at the bottom of the terrace. Thus, Michetti was the first to present the architectural design which when developed would lead to the creation of a masterpiece of Russian architecture.

Even the new palace, which stretched for 160 metres along the edge of the terrace, did not solve the problem of where to accommodate the growing court.

In 1747 with the blessing of Peter's daughter, the Empress Elizabeth, Bartolomeo Rastrelli embarked upon a radical rebuilding of the Upper Chambers. All that remained of the former building was the central section erected in Peter's time.

The new palace was built with unprecedented speed. By 1755 the décor was practically complete. The size and sumptuousness of the rooms, the remarkable skill of the architect and craftsmen astounded contemporaries.

Rastrelli retained the existing division of the palace into a central section with galleries and side buildings. But he added galleries that ran south in the direction of the Upper Gardens. He did away with the small pavilions at the east and west ends of the palace, replacing them by a "building under arms" (at the west end) and a "church building" (at the east end).

The palace interiors were in keeping with its external appearance. Its spacious and airy rooms were adorned with rich mouldings, splendid parquet flooring, exquisite carving, painted ceilings,

Great Palace

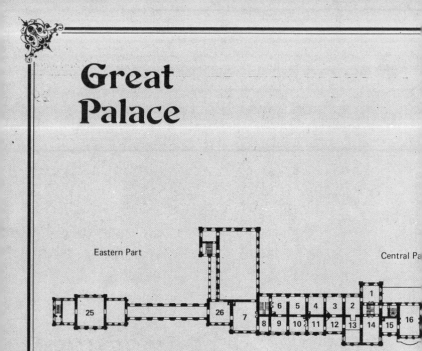

Eastern Part

Central Pa

1. Oak Study
2. Crown Room
3, 4, 5, 6. Spare Rooms
7. Great Blue Drawing Room
8. Intercommunicating Room
9. Cavalier Room
10. Intercommunicating

(Standard) Room
11. Empress's Study
12. Dressing Room
13. Divan Room
14. Partridge Drawing Room
15. East Chinese Room
16. Portrait Hall

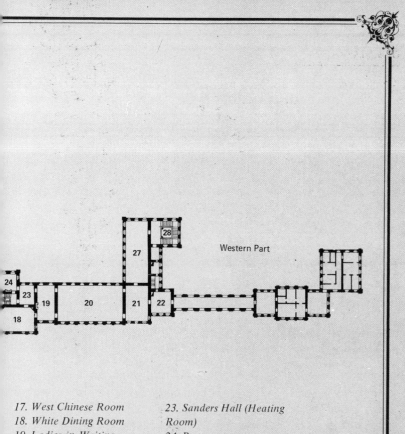

Western Part

17. *West Chinese Room*
18. *White Dining Room*
19. *Ladies-in-Waiting*
(Audience) Room
20. *Throne Room*
21. *Cheshma Room*
22. *Blue Reception Room*

23. *Sanders Hall (Heating*
Room)
24. *Pantry*
25. *Church*
26. *Secretary Room*
27. *Dance Hall*
28. *Grand Staircase*

32 and canvases by great masters. Rastrelli's interiors appeared in the last decade of Baroque, so many of them were not destined to last for long. In subsequent decades many famous architects with different architectural styles enriched the exterior and interiors of the Great Palace.

So alongside the rooms dating back to the Petrine period were the splendid halls that appeared in the mid-18th century and then the dignified, austere halls of the Classical period that were later replaced by the interiors of the mid-19th century reflecting a revival of the main artistic principles of Rococo.

It must be said that the architects who worked in the Great Palace showed considerable respect for the work of their predecessors. In some interiors the changes affected only certain sections of the walls. Rastrelli, for example, sometimes limited himself to the finish of panels and doorways and left the moulding and painting of the Petrine period unaltered, while Velten, who worked in the Classical style, deliberately left Rastrelli's carved ornament. Individual details that appeared in the mid-19th century in the old rooms blended well with the existing décor. Because this mixture of styles was the work of outstanding masters there is no trace of eclecticism here. On the contrary, the styles blend together in a remarkable way to form a complex and fascinating unity.

Over the two centuries of its existence the Great Palace has become a kind of treasure-store of outstanding works of art, furniture, bronzes, china, glass and everyday objects. Yet neither the architectural merits of the palace, nor the artistic merits of its collections were studied before 1917, nor were they preserved properly. It was practically impossible for specialists and art historians to gain admittance to this magnificent building.

After the victory of the October Socialist Revolution the Great Palace was made a museum open to the public. In the pre-war years it became one of the most popular museums in the Soviet Union.

The Nazis set fire to the Great Palace on the very first day of

Chinese Room

their occupation of Peterhof. The fire destroyed not only this world-famous gem of architecture, but also many works of art. Everything that survived the fire was either destroyed or looted. Not content with this, they blew up the north wall of the most valuable, Petrine section of the palace.

When Peterhof was liberated all that remained of the Great Palace were charred ruins.

The destruction was so great that many people considered it quite out of the question to even think of trying to restore the palace. The initial conservation work and measurements began almost as soon as the invaders were driven out. Parallel to this a careful study was made of archive material, designs and photographs.

A draft plan for the restoration of the exterior was drawn up in 1947, and the following year the Soviet Government authorised work to commence on the restoration of the interiors and setting up of the museum. The first stage in this highly complex task was the drawing up of a plan for restoration under the supervision of the architects Vassily Savkov and Yevgenia Kazanskaya.

First on the agenda was general construction work and restoration of the facades of the palace, including the intricately shaped roofs, the wrought-iron railings on the balconies, the stone mouldings and carvings, and the gilded coverings and ornament. All this took ten years.

The next stage was the restoration of the interiors. By this time Leningrad experts had acquired considerable experience in resurrecting cultural monuments. But the Great Palace, like any masterpiece of architecture, had certain unique features, which is why so many problems arose during its restoration.

In this connection it is hard to overestimate the importance of the research work that preceded restoration. This research made it possible to ascertain certain processes characteristic of the 18th century, the composition of the materials used, and the technology

50 of their manufacture and application, to establish authorship and to select similar works in order to reconstruct lost elements in the décor. The first rooms to be restored were opened to the public in 1963.

Highly complex though it was, the restoration of the interiors represented merely one stage of the work, for the Great Palace was also restored as a museum. The reassembling of the museum exhibits also demanded a great deal of hard work from the members of the team of experts. More than half the works of art that had adorned the palace before World War II could not be evacuated in time. Before the museum could be opened a lot of collecting had to be done. Objects that had left Peterhof at different times and in different circumstances had to be located and returned to their former places, and paintings and works of decorative and applied arts similar to those that had been lost had to be obtained from other museums. In several cases it was decided to replace lost objects with items the date and style of which were in keeping with the palace interiors. Only in exceptional cases, when replacement with similar objects was not possible, were replicas of the lost works of art made.

Today the Great Palace Museum numbers more than twenty rooms and its collection of exhibits is in no way inferior to the pre-war one. Let us begin our tour of the palace with the oldest part, built during the reign of Peter the Great.

VESTIBULE AND OAK STAIRCASE

Entering through the glass doors in the centre of the building and crossing the spacious vestibule with a marble floor, you pass through the archway in the west wall and reach the Oak Staircase, which was the Grand Staircase in the old Upper Chambers. The architect Jean-Baptiste Le Blond designed it as a rather narrow, three-flight staircase in keeping with the original, modest appearance of the chambers. The exquisite décor and the beautifully carved oak balusters by Nicolas Pineau make the Oak Staircase one of the most interesting specimens of Petrine architecture.

When another storey was added to the palace in the middle of the 18th century Rastrelli increased the size of the windows and the height of the room by making a large oval-shaped opening in the ceiling through which you could see the painting on the ceiling belonging to that period by Ivan Vishnyakov showing the goddess of the dawn, Aurora, in her chariot.

In 1978 restoration work on the Oak Staircase was completed. From a charred fragment of one of the balusters found during an examination of the palace ruins after the war and from existing photographs a model was reconstructed from which a fine new balustrade was carved. The ceiling was restored by the painter Yakov Kazakov from a black-and-white pre-war photograph and earlier descriptions.

On the west wall in a richly carved oak frame hangs a portrait of Peter the Great. It is thought to have been painted from life in 1716 by the Danish artist Benoît Coffre during a visit by Peter to Copenhagen.

OAK STUDY OF PETER THE GREAT

The Oak Staircase leads up to the first floor. Through the central hall is another room that retains for the most part the décor of the first quarter of the 18th century. This is the Oak Study of Peter the Great. Its splendid carving impressed even contemporaries. The study was decorated with oak panels and carved compositions designed by Le Blond. The carved compositions on the walls were the work of the sculptor Nicolas Pineau and his assistants in 1718-1720 from Pineau's own designs. Originally there were twelve wall compositions, one over the doorway, and those on the door itself. Their subjects were the four seasons, war trophies and musical

52 instruments. Two were idealised bas-reliefs of Peter the Great and, it is believed, his wife Catherine as Minerva, the goddess of wisdom. The panel over the door showed an incense-burner surrounded by winged dragons. The doors were decorated with herms. The superb compositions, fine detail, remarkable feeling for the material and lively execution make these panels a real masterpiece of decorative art.

In 1941 eight compositions, plus those over the doorway and on the door itself, were removed and evacuated. Everything that could not be sent to safety perished in the fire. The lost carved panels are at present being restored. Three of them (slightly lighter than the original ones) can be seen next to the original carved panels of the Petrine period. They were carved by Boris Gershelman with great skill from designs by Nadezhda Ode.

The furniture in the study is similar to that which was here before the war. Of particular interest is the German clock made at the beginning of the 18th century and thought to have belonged to Peter the Great.

CROWN ROOM

Adjoining the Oak Study to the east is a small suite of rooms of identical size facing south that appeared as a result of the addition of new buildings to the Petrine Upper Chambers by Rastrelli in 1747-1755. In the first of these rooms the only surviving element of the original décor is the parquet floor with the lively zigzag Baroque pattern found in many living rooms and halls of the palace.

In 1770 a deep alcove was made in this room from a design by Yuri Velten. In layout the room resembles a typical 18th-century royal bedchamber. Since it was linked by a corridor with an identical room in the opposite, empress's half of the palace, it may be assumed that this room was intended to be the emperor's bedchamber. Its first occupant, however, Paul I, did not make use of it until twenty-five years later. He requested the architect Vincenzo Brenna to design a special stand where the crown could be displayed while the emperor was in residence. Ever since then the room has been called the Crown Room.

Due to a lack of photographs, it was decided during the restoration of the interior to make use of Yuri Velten's own design that had survived in the archives of the Petrodvorets Museum. For the ceiling the restorers used a painting by an unknown, 18th-century French painter on the mythological subject of Venus and Adonis, a favourite theme in the décor of 18th-century interiors.

The early 18th-century Chinese silk covering the walls is interesting mainly because it depicts the various stages in the manufacture of Chinese porcelain.

The carved gilded four-poster bed is characteristic of 18th-century royal bedchambers and probably the work of an Italian master. The two inlaid commodes by the walls were made in South Germany in the middle of the 18th century.

The four rooms next to the Crown Room were not on display before the war although with a few changes they still retained Rastrelli's décor. Having no fixed purpose and being used partly for accommodating guests, they have long been referred to as the "spare rooms".

Restoration work is now being carried out in these rooms. For the time being they contain exhibits relating to the history of the palace.

SECRETARY ROOM

This was also called the Choir Antechamber, because a door led from it to a gallery terrace along which you could reach the palace Church of SS Peter and Paul.

Rastrelli decorated the panels with carved and gilded ornament and covered the walls with silk. In the south-west corner was a stove covered with tiles showing blue cobalt drawings of landscapes. There were abundant supplies of these tiles in the palace store-houses. Stoves of different patterns and sizes were assembled from standard parts. The architect usually produced a very general design from which the master put the stove together with certain variations. The Secretary Room stove was reconstructed in 1981, the pattern on the tiles being reproduced from pre-war photographs and fragments found in the palace ruins.

The silk for the walls was made by Soviet weavers from a specimen corresponding to the type and colouring of 19th-century silk.

The inlaid desks and tables are Russian and Dutch work. The china vases were made in St Petersburg in the 19th century. The chandelier holding 48 candles is of great value. It was made for the Great Palace in the summer of 1851 at the Imperial Porcelain Works in St Petersburg. The painting on it is thought to be the work of Fyodor Krasovsky.

GREAT BLUE DRAWING ROOM

This spacious room is the first of a sumptuous suite of rooms that run the full length of the Great Palace from west to east. Standing at the point where the main section of the building adjoined the west wing, which contained the living chambers, this room was designed by Rastrelli to serve when necessary as a private dining room for the family or a small number of guests.

The walls with carved and gilded wooden panels were originally hung with raspberry-coloured silk.

The silk was changed several times until the walls were hung with blue fabric in the latter half of the 19th century. Since then the room has been known as the Blue Drawing Room. Its special status in relation to the other living quarters is stressed by its higher ceiling in comparison with the surrounding interiors.

It contains a banqueting service for official receptions made in 1849-1853 at the Imperial Porcelain Works in St Petersburg. Craftsmen at the same factory produced the china chandelier and large gold and cobalt painted vases in 1848.

There are two huge, impressive portraits on the wall, one of Elizabeth II, a copy of a portrait by Dmitri Levitsky, and the other of Paul I's wife Maria, the work of Vigée-Lebrun.

SMALLER INTERCOMMUNICATING ROOM

This is remarkable for the beautiful pattern and rich colour of the mid-19th-century silk wall hangings made specially for Peterhof at the Grigory Sapozhnikov manufactory in Moscow. Many spare rolls of it were kept in the museum's storerooms before the war and evacuated to safety, making it possible to cover all the walls in the room with it.

Of the pictures the most interesting are the portrait of an old man in Oriental dress by Giandomenico Tiepolo (1696-1770), the portrait of the 16th-century Italian poetess Vittoria Accoramboni by Scipione Pulzone (1550-1597), the *Architectural Landscape* by an unknown 17th-century German painter and the *Nymphs by the Spring,* also by an unknown German artist of the second half of the 18th century.

CAVALIER ROOM

The room is so called because the Cavalier Guards responsible for guarding the Empress's private apartments used to do sentry duty here. The walls are hung with raspberry-coloured fabric woven from a pre-war specimen that survived. The carved and gilded décor is in the process of being restored.

The exhibits in the Cavalier Room have no direct functional significance. They consist mainly of items of mahogany furniture

56 made by 18th-century English masters. The splendid inlaid cabinet and bureau with scenes *à la chinoiserie* made in South Germany belong to roughly the same period.

Of the pictures the most interesting are *The Horrors of War* from the workshop of Rubens after his late work painted in 1638, the *Episode des guerres de Louis XIV en Flandre* by the famous painter of battle-pieces Adam Frans van der Meulen, court painter to Louis XIV, the *Cavalry Charge* by the 17th-century master Jacques Courtois, nicknamed Le Bourguignon, and *Combats de cavalérie,* the work of an unknown 18th-century Dutch master.

INTERCOMMUNICATING ROOM

In old palace inventories this room is called by a different name, the Standard Room. This is explained either by the custom of keeping in here the standards of the guards regiments stationed in Peterhof during the summer, or by the colour of the wall hangings, yellow, which was also the colour of the Imperial standard. However, the function of the room, which came just before the private apartments, is more in keeping with the frequently used name of an intercommunicating room.

The most interesting item of furniture here is the inlaid folding card-table decorated with a wide selection of different types of wood in marquetry technique. The top and lower section of the table have inlaid representations of architectural edifices and whole landscapes. This table is mentioned in all the surviving palace inventories. The fact that the Great Palace collection contains another two tables identical to this in size, proportions and marquetry technique suggests the existence of a workshop in St Petersburg in the 1760s specially commissioned by the palace.

The private rooms in the female section of an 18th-century Russian palace invariably contained a study, dressing room, bed-chamber and boudoir.

The term "study" did not mean that the occupant engaged in matters of state here. Often people just dropped in here to have a game of cards among a close circle of intimates. But the furnishing of the study had to give the appearance of serious occupations. In fact the décor of this room, designed by Rastrelli, was just the same as that of the neighbouring rooms: the same silk on the walls and gilded wooden carving on the doors and panels of the skirting board. The décor was destroyed when the palace was set on fire in 1941.

Today the walls are hung with white satin patterned with baskets of flowers, the same silk that hung here throughout the 19th century. It probably goes back to a French Lyonese silk manufactured in the 1760s and 1770s and later reproduced in Russian factories.

The study, like most of the rooms in the living quarters of the palace, was always adorned with portraits. It was a kind of family portrait gallery, although it also contained portraits of European monarchs. Peterhof for the most part contained copies or author's replicas of famous originals by West European painters.

The 18th-century portraits are of interest: Catherine the Great by Vigilius Erichsen, King Stanislaw Poniatowski of Poland by Pietro Rotari, the Empress Elizabeth by an unknown Russian painter, and a portrait of the Empress Maria Fyodorovna painted in 1801 by Gerhard Kügelgen.

The splendid gilt chairs and divan were made in the workshop of Georges Jacob, one of the most famous French furniture-makers of the second half of the 18th century. The secretaire by the west wall is the work of David Röntgen, a German furniture-maker who worked at the French court.

DRESSING ROOM

This room is the same size as the study. The silk with which the walls are hung was taken from spare rolls saved by evacuation. It was made in the mid-19th century at the Sapozhnikov brothers' manufactory specially for the Great Palace.

The Dressing Room exhibits are almost exactly what they were before 1941. Of special interest is the mirror in a superb silver frame with exquisite detail. A notice tells us that the frame was the work of the eminent mid-18th century French jeweller, François Thomas Germain. The Russian coat-of-arms at the top suggests that the mirror was a present to the Empress Elizabeth from Louis XV of France.

The portrait of the Empress Elizabeth painted by Charles van Loo, one of the finest portrait painters at the court of Louis XV, hanging over the dressing table, was also a present.

On the opposite wall is a portrait of the Empress Elizabeth, mounted on a horse, with an Arab boy standing beside her. This is another version by Georg Grooth of his painting that was popular in the 1740s.

DIVAN ROOM

The Royal Bedchamber, which became known as the Divan Room in the latter half of the 18th century, is in the north-east protruding part of the central section of the palace. Here the architectural emphasis is shifted to the south wall, a wooden wall with an alcove as in the Crown Room with which the Divan Room was connected by a passage on the left of the niche. The wooden wall is decorated with beautifully traced and gilded ornament and two haut-relief cupids peeping out playfully from the apertures over the doors by the alcove. The bedchamber received this décor in 1770 when Rastrelli's interior was reconstructed by the architect Yuri Velten.

In accordance with European court ritual of the 17th and first half of the 18th century the Royal Bedchamber was the most honoured of all the rooms in the palace. The monarch's retiring and rising were treated as important acts of state. And the Bedchamber was rightfully included in the suite of state apartments.

In the second half of the 18th century, however, court life became somewhat less formal, and the private apartments acquired a more intimate character. First a splendid four-poster bed appeared in the alcove of the bedchamber, to be replaced shortly afterwards by a large Turkish divan.

As in the Crown Room a great deal of work went into the restoration and replacement of lost sections of the Chinese silk on the walls. Of the objects that have been in the Divan Room for a long time the most interesting are the portrait of the Empress Elizabeth as a child, a copy by the 18th-century artist Heinrich Buchholz of the work by the French painter Louis Caravacque, the egg-shaped china vase made at the Imperial Porcelain Works in the middle of the 18th century, and the remarkably life-like sculpture of Catherine II's favourite Italian greyhound Zemira lying on a cushion, a replica made in 1770 of the work by the French sculptor Jean Dominique Rachette.

PARTRIDGE DRAWING ROOM

One is immediately struck by the similarity of this room to the previous one. It has three windows, and the south wall consists of a wooden partition with a niche. True, the niche is shaped somewhat differently and is intended for a gently curving divan. The walls are hung with pale-blue silk patterned with wreaths and flower garlands, ears of corn and leaves forming a kind of trellis. There is also a repeating

60   pattern of partridges running about in the grass. It is from this that the room gets its name.

The abundance of light and gilt, the rich colour of the silk and the warm shades of the parquet flooring give the Partridge Drawing Room a special radiance and freshness.

This room, originally decorated from a design by Rastrelli and later redecorated by Velten, was intended as a boudoir where morning occupations and conversations took place in an intimate circle in close proximity to the bedchamber. The silk hangings, made around 1770 in Lyons, the centre of the French silk-weaving industry, under the supervision of Philippe de Lassalle, were just right for this atmosphere. Lassalle's work was well known in Europe and eagerly purchased for Russian palaces. At the beginning of the 19th century the Lyonese silk was replaced by Russian silks woven at a Moscow factory.

The silk now covering the walls was made in the 1960s at the Moscow Silk Research Institute from a surviving specimen. The west wall is hung with remains from the pre-war store. A comparison of the old and new silk reveals the skill of the modern weavers.

The painting on the ceiling by an unknown 18th-century French artist, an allegorical representation of Morning driving away Night, is also in keeping with the room's function.

Formerly the Partridge Drawing Room was hung with portraits of the first girls to study at the Smolny Institute founded by Catherine II. They were painted by the gifted Russian artist of the late 18th and early 19th century Dmitri Levitsky. At the beginning of this century the portraits were presented to the Russian Museum. A copy made by the 19th-century artist Heinrich Schmidt of Levitsky's portrait of Yekaterina Nelidova, a graduate from the Institute, hangs on the east wall as a reminder of the room's former ornament. On the opposite wall are portraits of girls' heads painted by Jean-Baptiste Greuze (1725-1805) and an 18th-century copy of his canvas *An Allegory of Fidelity.*

The furniture of the Partridge Drawing Room consists mostly of 18th-century items. The inlaid wardrobe standing by the west wall was probably manufactured in the 1760s in the workshop of the English furniture-maker Cobb. It is one of the few items of furniture from the Great Palace that were saved from the Nazis.

The harp in the middle of the room was made in the first half of the 19th century in the London workshop of the famous French musical instrument-maker Sebastian Erard.

CHINESE ROOMS

The two Chinese rooms, the East and the West, are arranged symmetrically on either side of the Great Palace. Their rich décor (lacquered wall panels, ceilings painted in imitation of china, and extremely complex patterns on the parquet floors) were intended to impress, to carry one off into the realm of the exotic, the mysterious, remote lands of the Orient.

In 1766-1769 Jean-Baptiste Vallin de la Mothe decorated the walls of two rooms in the Great Palace with panels from old lacquered Chinese screens showing scenes of mustering troops, setting out on campaigns, rice harvesting, and landscapes. The lower panels, skirting boards, door sections and ceilings were painted "in Chinese style" by the Russian master Fyodor Vlassov. Thus it was that the Chinese rooms appeared.

The painting in the rooms was destroyed during the war and restored in the 1960s and 1970s by a team of Leningrad specialists under Leonid Lyubimov using the two surviving Chinese panels saved by evacuation, plus some water colours of the rooms and black-and-white photographs. The quality of their work can be judged from the gold medal which the Academy of Arts of the USSR awarded them.

The parquet floors presented considerable difficulties for the restorers, for they consisted of unusual pictures made up of thousands of different coloured pieces of rare types of wood. The decorators under Boris Mitskevich made a fine job of restoring the tiled stoves which in terms of complexity of shape and artistic treatment had no analogy in Russian palaces. Today these fine specimens of ceramic art adorn the Chinese rooms once more.

The most interesting items on display today in the cabinets are the English mid-18th century lacquered desk and chairs (East Room), a French bureau of the 1770s and some Chinese rosewood chairs (West Room) of the same period. Also of interest is the collection of Chinese porcelain from the Imperial Works in the town of Jingdezhen and the Japanese porcelain made in the town of Arita specially for export to Europe. Note also the bright baffled and painted enamel from Canton and lacquered boxes from Peking.

PORTRAIT HALL

In the middle of the oldest section of the palace is a large hall with windows on either side, some facing the parterre of the Upper Gardens, others the Great Cascade and Marine Canal of the Lower Park. After the relatively small rooms of the living quarters this hall seems particularly large and sunny. At one time it was the largest room in the Upper Chambers built in Peter's lifetime and was simply called the Hall. Its décor dates back to the period when Le Blond was chief architect of Peterhof. It was probably on his initiative that the floor was tiled with black and white marble in a checkered pattern.

On the west and east walls facing each other were two fireplaces with mirrors. The walls had friezes with three recurring moulded compositions symbolising scholarship, the art of warfare, navigation and the arts. The décor was completed by oak panels running along the lower sections of the walls and four Gobelin tapestries.

In 1723 the artist Bartolomeo Tarsia, who came to Russia from Italy, presented Peter the Great with a sketch for painting the ceiling of the Hall. Peter approved it. The artist was not able to carry out the work until after the Emperor's death, in 1726. The subject of the painting was the flowering of Russia under its wise sovereign. When the palace was rebuilt Rastrelli decorated the panels, doors and window recesses with intricate gilded carving which Russian masters under Joseph Stahlmeyer reproduced from models by Louis Rolland.

In 1764 the walls were hung with no less than 368 paintings acquired on the orders of Catherine II from the widow of the Italian painter Pietro Rotari who died in St Petersburg. Most of them are portraits of girls in various costumes painted by the artist and his pupils. Ever since then the Hall has been called the Picture or Portrait Hall, and sometimes the Room of Modes and Graces.

The central section of the Great Palace suffered most in the war. After setting fire to it the invaders blew up the north wall of the Picture Hall. Only a few small fragments of the frieze moulding remained. But the collection of paintings was preserved in its entirety by being evacuated, and this encouraged the idea of the need to restore the interior. It was with the restoration of the Picture Hall that the work of resurrecting the Great Palace began.

On the mantelpieces of the fireplaces are splendid bronze clocks made by French masters in the second half of the 18th century. The two fireplace surrounds, or trivets, as they are called, are masterpieces of French bronze plastic art of the mid-18th century, particularly the west fireplace, which shows Venus and Vulcan. The grand piano was made in Moscow in 1794 by Johann Stumpff.

WHITE DINING ROOM

In 1774-1775 this room was given a typical Classical décor designed by the architect Velten. The large smooth wall panels bear haut-relief compositions of hunting trophies, gardening tools, etc. The wall surfaces are decorated with heavy mouldings of flower garlands and bunches of grapes. Subjects from Greek mythology were used in the ornament of this hall, as in the earlier interiors.

After the rebuilding of the 1770s the Hall became known as the White Dining Room. It was used for sumptuous formal banquets. The dinner service on display here was used on such occasions for many years. It was made in England in 1770 from cream-coloured "Queen's ware" at the Etruria factory owned by Josiah Wedgwood. More than 196 items of the original service have survived. Some of the replacements were made at Russian factories. The glass exhibited with the china was made in Russia and Bohemia in the 18th century.

AUDIENCE ROOM

This room, which was also known as the Ladies-in-Waiting Room, remained unaltered right up to 1941, retaining Rastrelli's splendid ornament.

The architect introduced a huge composite order into the décor of the walls. The pilasters formed a kind of carcass. The spaces between them were taken up by double rows of windows, huge doors, or large windows and mock mirror windows.

The main work on the Audience Room was completed in 1753. At the beginning of the following year the Italian artist Paolo Ballarini, newly arrived from Italy, began painting the ceiling. He was assisted by the Russian masters Yakov Ligotsky and Fyodor Nesterov. Three months later the work was completed.

The theme of the ceiling painting was taken from the 16th-century Italian poet Torquato Tasso's *Jerusalem Delivered* (1580), which was very popular in the 18th century. The poem is about the First Crusade. One of its finest passages tells of the Christian knight Rinaldo's love for the Saracen maiden Armida. Ballarini depicted the moment when Rinaldo is imploring Armida not to kill herself, but to become his wife.

During the war there was no time to evacuate the painting and it was destroyed by fire. All the Soviet restorers Leonid Lyubimov and Vladimir Nikiforov had to help them reconstruct it was one black-and-white photograph and some written descriptions. Not a single work by Ballarini had survived either in the Soviet Union or in the painter's homeland. The restoration of the painting took more than two years.

Even more laborious was the work of restoring the carved and gilded ornament. This was the first room in the Great Palace that had needed to have the whole of Rastrelli's décor restored. The carving and gilding were completed by 1973.

THRONE ROOM

In 1777-1778 Velten provided a new décor for the hall, the largest chamber in the palace. It was here that official receptions, large banquets and, of course, balls were held. The abundance of light from the twenty-eight windows arranged in two rows made the room particularly imposing. Because a throne was often put here for official receptions, the room became known as the Throne Room.

Velten made the east wall where the throne stood the focal point of the décor. He hung a huge portrait here of Catherine the Great on horseback painted by the Danish artist Vigilius Erichsen in 1762. Right and left of the portrait the architect put two large bas-reliefs by the sculptor Ivan Prokofiev symbolising the principles of the "enlightened monarch" that the Empress considered herself to be, *Justice* and *Truth and Virtue*. Above it is a bas-relief by Mikhail Kozlovsky entitled *The Return of Svyatoslav After His Victory Over the Pechenegs* and *The Baptism of Grand Princess Olga* by Arkhip Ivanov.

The theme of the first relief is the victory of a Russian host. The second subject pointed clearly to the role of woman in the life of the Russian state and recalled the baptism of Catherine herself into the Russian Orthodox faith. The large portraits of Russian empresses by Heinrich Buchholz over the doorways testify to the tradition of women acceding to the Russian throne.

Between the upper windows Velten hung portraits of both close and distant relatives of Peter the Great, whose portrait can be seen above the doorway in the south-west corner.

An important role in the décor of the Throne Room, used for receiving foreign embassies, was assigned to four huge paintings on the west wall depicting scenes from the Battle of Cheshma (1770) by the Englishman Richard Paton. This great sea victory by Russia over the Turkish fleet was a most vivid and glorious page in Russian 18th-century history, and the pictures were intended to remind people of it.

During World War II the paintings by Richard Paton and Heinrich Buchholz were evacuated. In the 1960s Vigilius Erichsen's portrait of Catherine the Great was found and restored to its former place. The throne by the east wall was made in the early 18th century by Russian masters and is thought to have belonged to Peter the Great.

The official opening of the Throne Room after restoration took place in 1969.

Whereas Paton's pictures form only part of the décor of the Throne Room, in the neighbouring room battle scenes are the focal point. Twelve paintings of sea battles during the Russo-Turkish War of 1768-1774 take up three walls in the room, which is a kind of monument to Russian naval prowess. These canvases belong to the brush of the German painter Philippe Hackert and were commissioned by the Russian government in 1771-1772. In 1779 Velten hung them here in two rows after providing them with unusual moulded frames. Over the doorways he placed bas-reliefs of Turkish trophies.

Hackert's pictures show scenes from various stages of the war, but the most popular canvases were those depicting the battle between a Russian squadron and the Turkish fleet in Cheshma Bay in the Aegean in 1770. This battle became known as the Battle of Cheshma, hence the name of the room.

During World War II the canvases were evacuated. Before being returned to their former places, they were restored by the Soviet artists Rudolf Sausen and Boris Kosenkov.

The ceiling was attractively painted by the German artist Augustin Terwesten in 1690 with *The Sacrifice of Iphigenia,* a scene from the Trojan War.

The mahogany furniture here was made by Russian masters in the first third of the 19th century. The marble busts of Catherine the Great and her favourite Grigory Orlov were made in Carrara by the Italian sculptor Giovanni Cibei in the second half of the 18th century.

BLUE RECEPTION ROOM

The room next to the Cheshma Room was an auxiliary one. Decorated from a design by Rastrelli, it resembled the interiors of

68   the south half of the palace used as spare rooms—carved panels, silk hangings, and a zigzag design on the parquet flooring. The room got its name from the colour of the silk on the walls.

The items in the room are typical of the décor of state apartments. The paintings on the walls include three showing the Great Palace and the Great Cascade, all belonging to the first half of the 19th century. The ceiling painting on a mythological subject was chosen from the Hermitage collection. It is the work by an unknown 18th-century French artist.

Of the items of furniture the most valuable is the mahogany bureau with marble columns. It was made in St Petersburg at the beginning of the 19th century in the workshop of the furniture-maker Heinrich Gambs.

The door from the Cheshma Room leads into the Dance Hall, or Merchants' Hall as it was also called. Restoration work is still in progress here and on the Grand Staircase as well. It is also planned to restore the Church building and the East Wing. A great deal of complex work still has to be done to resurrect treasures that seemed to have been lost forever.

Lower
Park

From the terrace by the north facade of the Great Palace you have a splendid view of the Lower Park covering an area of more than 100 hectares and the sea. The focal point is the Great Cascade. Right and left of it are the Grand Flower-beds with the Chalice Fountains. In front of the Cascade in the middle of the basin the mighty jet of the Samson Fountain shoots into the air. From there the water of the Cascade flows along the canal, straight as an arrow, to the sea. The canal divides the park into two more or less equal parts, usually called the west and east sections. The east section contains the Monplaisir Palace, the Chess Hill Cascade, the Pyramid Fountain, the Sun Fountain and the Jester Fountains, etc.

The west section contains the Hermitage Pavilion and the Château de Marly, the Golden Hill and Lion cascades, the Menagerie Fountain and the Triton Fountains.

On Peter the Great's instructions work began in 1714 on a complex network of avenues, squares with flower-beds, basins and fountains on the marshy shore of the Gulf of Finland. The specialist Leonardt van Harnigfelt was invited from Holland to supervise it. It was he who trained the team of fine Russian specialists that created this splendid specimen of a formal Baroque garden.

The drawings of the mathematician and cartographer Saint-Hilaire compiled in the early 1770s show the Lower Park at its finest. Tastes changed quickly, however, and with them the Lower Park changed too. The trees and shrubs ceased to be trimmed, the intricate shapes of the potted plants disappeared, the patterns of the flower-beds were spoilt, and to some extent the layout as a whole, many pavilions were removed, and even some of the fountains. The period of "decline" lasted until the beginning of the 20th century.

The first attempts to restore individual sections of the Peterhof parks were made in the pre-war period, but the subsequent destruction of Peterhof by the Nazis caused what seemed to be irreparable damage to the parks. However, the work started as early as 1945 aimed at restoring the original, formal character of the Lower Park. The 1,050 limes planted in the Marly Avenue at that time now form a clear, straight line.

In the 1960s a plan was drawn up for the complete restoration of the Lower Park. It will help to restore the park to its 18th-century appearance depicted by Saint-Hilaire. It is not just a matter of restoring the surviving fountains and pavilions, but of recreating those that have been lost, replacing unhealthy trees and trimming new trees and shrubs to give them proportions and shapes in keeping with the original design.

GREAT CASCADE

This central point in the impressive system of fountains was planned by Peter the Great himself. In its dimensions, abundance of water, rich sculpture, variety of jet patterns and remarkable overall unity this splendid specimen of Baroque art is one of the finest fountain ensembles in the world. Forming a single whole with the Great Palace, the Cascade, the bowl at its feet and the Marine Canal also constitute the north-south axis of the Lower Park. The sculpture reflects the main idea behind the Peterhof ensemble as a whole, the glorification of Russia's victories in her struggle for access to the Baltic.

The formal opening of the cascade took place in Peter's presence on 13 July, 1721. As yet it had no sculptural ornament. English masters undertook to make and deliver some ornament to St Peters-

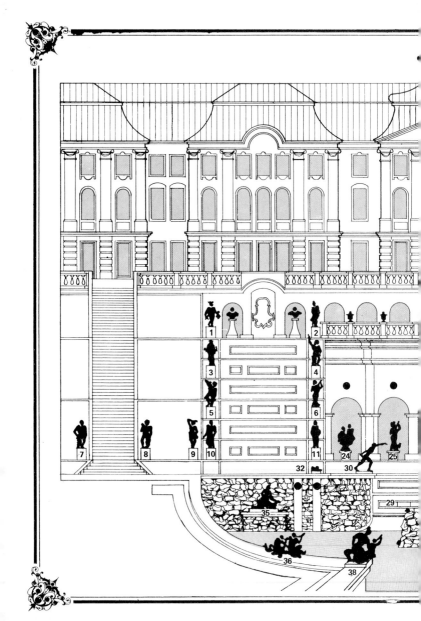

74 Great Cascade

1. Perseus
2. Pandora
3. Ceres
4. Capitoline Faun
5. Florentine Faun
6. Venus Caliphyga
7. Meleager
8. Bacchus with Satyr
9. Amazon
10. Jupiter
11. Capitoline Flora
12. Acis
13. Juno
14. Faun
15. Galatea
16. Medici Venus
17. Capitoline Mercury
18. Capitoline Antinous
19. Germanicus
20. Discus Thrower

21. Actaeon
22. Ganymede
23. Tritons
24. Pan and Apollo
25. Venus Caliphyga
26. Barberini Faun
27. Bacchus
28. Cupid and Psyche
29. Shell Fountains
30-31. Borghese Gladiators
32-33. Frogs
34. Volkhov
35. Neva
36. Sirens
38-39. Naiad with Dolphin
40. Samson
41. Half-figures of lions

burg by the end of the summer. This consisted mainly of bas-reliefs, corbels, pilasters, mascarons and other decorative elements, together with the figures of tritons, naiads, dolphins, Neptune and Amphitrite, and two toads.

Eighteen months later figures of the twelve months and twelve vases were cast in Holland from designs by Niccolo Michetti on Peter's orders. Some sculptures, mascarons, bas-reliefs and vases were cast in St Petersburg by Bartolomeo Rastrelli and François Vassé. By August 1723 all the pieces of sculpture had been gilded, and the Great Cascade began to play.

But work did not stop. Shortly afterwards the figures of Perseus, Actaeon, Galatea and Mercury appeared, with new mascarons of Bacchus and Neptune. Part of Peter's design did not take shape until after his death. In 1738 a group of two tritons blowing into a shell by Rastrelli was set up in the Lower Grotto.

In 1799 it was decided to replace the cascade's lead sculpture by bronze sculpture, retaining as far as possible the original forms of the figures. This work, in which many eminent sculptors of the day took part, was completed by July 1806. The result was a unique ensemble which not only served the patriotic aim of the Petrine monument, to glorify Russia's victory in the Northern War (1700-1721), but did so on a very high artistic level.

Fourteen statues were made from plaster casts of Greek originals in the Academy of Arts. The figure of Bacchus was a replica of the famous original by Michelangelo.

Nine statues and one group were cast from original models by leading sculptors of the day, Feodosy Shchedrin, Jean-Dominique Rachette, Fedot Shubin, Ivan Prokofiev and Ivan Martos. Some figures (Perseus, Actaeon and Galatea) repeated the theme of the earlier statues but were completely independent, superb compositions, others introduced new themes—the reclining Neptune and Amphitrite were replaced by reclining Neva and Volkhov. New sculptures were also erected: Jupiter, Juno, Acis and Pandora. The Gladiators (free copies of the work by Borghese) were set up in place of the "Pistols". Their outstretched hands were gripping snakes with jets of water pouring out of their mouths.

The old lead bas-reliefs on the steps, Rastrelli's toads and mascarons were also preserved in part. The niches of the Upper Grotto were still adorned by four marble busts. Throughout the 19th century and the first half of the twentieth, the cascade underwent major repairs and rebuilding twice.

In the first few weeks after the Nazi invasion the most valuable sculptures of the Great Cascade were removed and either hidden in a tunnel that had remained since Peter the Great's day in the slope of the terrace or sent to Leningrad. Only the bas-reliefs, busts, mascarons and corbels, and the largest sculptures (the Triton, Neva and Volkhov) had to be left in place. When Peterhof was liberated, it was discovered that the Nazis had stolen them. Efforts to locate them were unsuccessful. They were recreated from models by Soviet sculptors in 1947-1950 and took their place in the resurrected cascade.

Today the Great Cascade can be viewed by guests to Peterhof in all its splendour: the 17 artificial waterfalls linked by five arches of the grotto, the 39 gilded bronze statues, the 29 bas-reliefs and the 142 jets of the 64 sprinklers. The restoration work shortly to be carried out will restore to this magnificent ensemble decorative elements lost over the many long years of its existence.

SAMSON FOUNTAIN

The largest fountain in the Lower Park is the Samson Fountain that stands in the centre of a bowl in front of the Great Cascade. Compositionally it crowns the fountain ensemble. The height of the sculptural group is 3.5 metres, and more than 6.5 metres including the pedestal. The giant Samson is wrenching apart the lion's jaws from which a twenty-metre-high jet shoots up. Eight gold dolphins send out jets at the giant's feet.

The decision to build the fountain was made in 1734 when the 25th anniversary of the Russian victory over the Swedes at Poltava was being celebrated. This highly important battle in the Northern War was fought on 27 June, 1709, St Samson's Day, which explains the allegorical representation of the victory in the form of Samson's victory over the lion. The lead sculpture was made in 1735 by Rastrelli.

Ten years later, however, this lead group was in need of restoration, and by the end of the 18th century it had to be replaced. One of the most distinguished sculptors of the day, Mikhail Kozlovsky, made use of the 18th-century composition to create a new model in Classical form of *Samson Wrenching Apart the Lion's Jaws* in which the heroic theme was felt even more strongly. In 1802 Kozlovsky's work, cast in bronze, was erected on a granite pedestal designed by the architect Andrei Voronikhin. In the niches at the foot of the pedestal are the heads of four lions facing the four points of the compass.

In 1941 there was no time to evacuate the sculpture, which weighed more than five tons. The Nazis stole it and, according to several accounts, melted it down for military purposes. In 1947 the Leningrad sculptor Vassily Simonov recreated Samson from pre-war drawings and photographs, and on 14 September of the same year the powerful figure again towered over the Lower Park, henceforth a symbol of the victory of civilisation over brutality.

TERRACE FOUNTAINS

On the terraces to the east and west of the Great Cascade are small white marble four-tiered cascades cut into the slope. On their upper walls the alternating mascarons of a Triton and nymphs glitter with gold. The water flowing from them comes from the fountains higher up on the ledge. Each cascade has a fountain with a circular marble bowl and a relatively low vertical jet.

The building of these fountains began in late 1799 and was completed by the middle of 1800. The cascades were faced with marble in 1852-1853. In all the job took about 740 tons of Carrara marble.

During the occupation the Terrace fountains were totally destroyed. They were restored by 1948.

CHALICE FOUNTAINS

Peter the Great's Field Journal contains the following entry for 8 July, 1721: "His Majesty dined at Monplaisir and after dinner turned on the water of the fountain by the Lower Flower-beds that adjoin the Upper Chambers." This was the first time a fountain played in Peterhof. It is the one still standing in the middle of the west flower-bed. The pipes and bowl were made by the Italian brothers Giovanni and Giuliano Barattini. The fountain in the east flower-bed was built by the Frenchman Paul Sualem, and was called the French fountain to distinguish it from the west one, known as the Italian fountain.

In 1854 craftsmen at the Peterhof Lapidary Works made the chalices and flowers of marble from a design by Andrei Stakenschneider using material left over from the building of the St Isaac's Cathedral in St Petersburg. Since there were no large slabs, each chalice of about 3.5 metres in diameter and weighing more than 16 tons was made of 49 pieces of marble skilfully carved and fitted together.

The Chalices play an important part in the fountain decoration of the central section of the Lower Park, providing compositional support for the Samson jet and organising the area of the Grand Flower-beds.

VORONIKHIN COLONNADES

On the east and west sides of the Marine Canal are marble colonnades and pavilions with gilded domes. The roofs of these structures have three vases with jets spurting out of them. The water splashes down the domes into semicircular marble basins, forming a kind of veil over the pavilion windows. The colonnades provide a fitting crown to this section of the park.

These Empire-style colonnades were erected in place of the wooden balustrade of the Petrine period by the architect Andrei

Voronikhin in 1803. The four pairs of lions by the staircase were carved from models by Ivan Prokofiev. The grey marble columns were brought from the Catherine Park of Tsarskoye Selo (now the town of Pushkin) and complemented with four columns of grey granite.

In 1853-1854 Andrei Stakenschneider faced the columns with Carrara and Sienna marble and decorated the floors with Venetian mosaic.

MARBLE SEAT FOUNTAINS

In the north-west and north-east corners of the Grand Flower-beds are huge semicircular seats of white Carrara marble made in 1853-1856 from a design by Andrei Stakenschneider. Their backs are decorated with curved lines, and their scroll-shaped arms end in large lion's paws.

Behind the seats on high cylindrical pedestals are shallow marble fountain bowls with discharge outlets in the form of lion's heads. In the middle of the bowl the architect has placed gilded female figures, a copy of the antique marble fountain statue of the *Nymph* in the Hermitage by the west seat and a copy of Christian Rauch's well-known *Danae* by the east seat.

MARINE CANAL

The north-south axis of the Lower Park is formed by the granite-faced walls of the Marine Canal, one of the oldest constructions in Peterhof. It begins at the harbour, out in the Gulf, and ends at the foot of the Great Cascade.

The digging of the canal began in 1715. Its construction was not dictated by artistic considerations alone. First and foremost, it was the official approach to the park. In spring and autumn, and in rainy summers, it was far more difficult to reach Peterhof along the muddy roads from St Petersburg than by sea. By the beginning of 1721 the work was completed for the most part. A contemporary eyewitness of the official opening of the residence in August 1721 wrote that the canal was 500 metres long and could take 115 vessels at a time. To deal with the gradient, Peter the Great ordered the engineer Vassily Tuvolkov to build a sluice 40 metres long and as high as the rising of the water—3 metres. The sluice had one chamber and was closed with oak gates. Two bascule bridges designed by Peter were built over the canal.

In the post-war period the canal walls have been faced with granite. A deeper harbour has been built making it possible for large vessels to dock in Peterhof. Today, as in the 18th century, many visitors come here by sea.

AVENUE OF FOUNTAINS

Along the Marine Canal Peter had trellises built with recesses in which it was proposed to build twenty-two fountains with sculptures based on Aesop's fables. The didactic message of the fables could easily be connected with the events of the Northern War.

In 1723 "The Two Snakes", "The Mountain that Gave Birth to a Mouse", "The Hen and the Kite" and "The Snake that Bit an Anvil" appeared in semicircular recesses. Each fountain had a notice explaining the meaning of the sculpture. The following year, however, Peter decided to construct the remaining fountains in the shape of vases with shallow bowls. With time the vases fell into disrepair, and in 1854-1860 they were removed, together with the sculpture of the Aesopian fountains. Craftsmen of the Peterhof Lapidary Works faced the fourteen south fountains on either side of the Marine Canal with Carrara marble. Only the intricate shapes of the eight stone pools near the sluice recall the earlier Baroque fountains.

The powerful jets from each of the basins form an unusual colonnade that leads up to the main cascade of Peterhof.

Samson Fountain

Triton and Turtle
Conservatory Fountain

Grand Conservatory

Monplaisir Palace.
Gallery and Lacquered
Study

Ceremonial Hall

Bedroom

Pyramid Fountain

Château de Marly   An interior in Château
                      de Marly

Shell Fountain

This fountain standing behind Voronikhin's west colonnade gives us an idea of what the 18th-century Aesopian fountains looked like. In a shallow basin four ducks go round in a circle chased by a little dog. The whole scene is accompanied by "barking" and "quacking". This fable is explained by the following notice: "The little dog Favourite is chasing the ducks on the water; the ducks are saying to it: 'It's no good. You have the strength to chase us, but not the strength to catch us!' "

The fountain was built by Paul Sualem in 1725 and commissioned by Catherine I. It had a special water wheel under the basin that made the figures move. From three pairs of bellows the air travelled along pipes to the figures carved by Nicolas Pineau and passed through mouthpieces with special metal strips that produced the "barks" and "quacks". Five years later Jakob Förster produced an automatic sound device.

During the war the fountain was destroyed by the Nazis. All that remained of its sculpture were the figures of the ducks found at the bottom of the Marine Canal. It was restored in 1957 with exactly the same mechanism as before. The sounds are produced with the help of a tape recording, however.

GRAND CONSERVATORY

To the east of the Grand Flower-beds is an oval garden with flowers, fruit trees, and a fountain in the middle. It is adjoined to the south by the richly decorated facade of the Conservatory. Its large windows, pilasters, mansard roof and balustrade with vases, the two-storey central section and two pavilions on either side give this building a palatial appearance. It was built in 1722-1725 from a design by Johann Friedrich Braunstein and Mikhail Zemtsov.

In the middle of the 18th century the Conservatory was considerably extended by the addition of side buildings. Russia's finest

106 gardeners worked here, growing grapes, melons, citrus fruits, etc.

The Grand Conservatory survived in this form until 1941. During the occupation the Nazis destroyed it almost completely. The building was restored from a design by Vassily Savkov in 1954. Today it is used as a rest centre.

CONSERVATORY (TRITON) FOUNTAIN

In the centre of the Conservatory garden in a circular basin is a gilded fountain group showing a huge Triton forcing apart the jaws of a sea monster. Four turtles are crawling away from the scene of the combat to the four points of the compass. A mighty jet of water is spurting from the monster's jaws. It blends in with the jets of four sprinklers spurting from the raised turtle heads. In its sculptural ornament this fountain, built in 1726 from a design by the architect Timofei Usov, has much in common with the Samson fountain. Like the latter, it has allegorical significance and is dedicated to the victory over the Swedish fleet in July 1714 by the Hangö Peninsula. The sculptural group was cast in lead from a model by Rastrelli. During the war the Nazis destroyed the fountain and dispatched the sculpture to Germany. Efforts to locate it have been unsuccessful.

In 1956 the sculptor Alexei Gurzhy reconstructed the original plastic ornament of the Conservatory fountain from a drawing in an 18th-century album.

ADAM AND EVE FOUNTAINS

At the point of where the two avenues running obliquely from the Grand Flower-beds to the sea cross Marly Avenue there are two identical fountains. The intersecting avenues form small squares with eight paths radiating from them. These squares which are equidistant to the west and east of the Marine Canal form an important element in the original layout of the Lower Park. And it is no accident that two of the park's earliest fountains, the Adam and Eve fountains, were built here.

The statues, free copies of the well-known works by Antonio Rizzi which still adorn the Doge's Palace in Venice, were commissioned from the sculptor Giovanni Bonazza in 1717 by Peter the Great's agent in Italy Savva Raguzinsky.

Adam and Eve arrived at Peterhof at the same time, but a place in the park was found for Adam only. Twenty days after the opening of the canal supplying water to Peterhof, Peter ordered that work begin on the building of the fountain. The design was by Niccolo Michetti and the work was supervised by Johann Friedrich Braunstein. The fountain was completed in 1722. At the same time four trellises were erected around it giving architectural shape to this area of the park.

On 25 July, 1925, after Peter's death, his widow and successor Catherine I ordered the building of the Eve fountain. It was designed by the architect Timofei Usov and began to play in the autumn of 1726.

In the early days of the Nazi invasion the Adam and Eve statues were buried in the Lower Park and thus escaped destruction. The fountains began to work again in 1948. Today they are all that remains of the original sculptural décor of the Petrine period.

Monplaisir

On the east side of the Lower Park a high rectangular artificial terrace fortified with granite juts out into the sea. Along its ridge runs a white stone balustrade behind which stands a single-storey brick building with a high, multi-tiered roof. The central building is flanked by two galleries that end in pavilions. The north walls of the galleries have narrow windows alternating with semicircular niches that emphasise the thickness of the walls battered by the north wind. From the south the galleries resemble a light arcade with streams of light flowing through the glass doors and windows. On this side there is an attractive garden with flower-beds and fountains. Nearby are the Bathing Pools and Steam Baths, the Assembly Hall with servants' rooms and a large building known as the Catherine Palace.

The whole of this ensemble, that took shape for the most part in the mid-18th century, is called Monplaisir, which is French for "my pleasure". The name really belongs to the small palace of which Peter the Great was so fond, one of the first buildings of Peterhof. Peter chose its site himself and drew up the plans for it. And wherever the Emperor happened to be, even if it was visiting abroad, he sent detailed instructions for the décor of the Monplaisir palace interiors. The building and interior decoration was supervised by Johann Friedrich Braunstein.

Construction of the palace began on 17 May, 1714. Two years later its central section was completed, and by August 1723, when the first large-scale celebrations were held in Peterhof, Monplaisir was completely finished.

In Peter's lifetime the palace was used for small receptions, dinners or suppers of an intimate nature. On 15 August, 1725 Catherine I held an official reception in Monplaisir in honour of the members of the St Petersburg Academy of Sciences founded in 1724.

In the middle of the 18th century Monplaisir began to lose its former importance, and although some modest entertaining was still done here, it turned, to quote the famous critic Vissarion Belinsky, into one of the most revered relics of Russian history. Unfortunately, the revering of Monplaisir did not extend to preserving the palace and its collections. The building gradually fell into disrepair, the silks mouldered with the damp, the pewter tarnished, the glass grew dim, and the paintings, of which there were more than two hundred in the palace, were spoilt.

Their fate was a sad one. Unheated during the winter and exposed to damp spring and autumn winds, Monplaisir was not an ideal repository for paintings. The restoration of pictures carried out here in 1746 and later can hardly be called professional. It was often thought best to simply replace a defective painting with another taken from the storeroom. When the water rose the rooms were sometimes flooded, causing considerable damage to the collection.

On 2 June, 1918 Monplaisir was opened to the public, and shortly afterwards planned restoration work began. The collection of paintings was carefully studied, restored and made good with pictures obtained from other museums and similar to those in the original collection. When the Nazis invaded, the art collection was evacuated, but the palace itself suffered greatly from the occupation. All the wooden details of the décor were burnt, the Dutch tiles on the walls smashed, the furnishings and lacquered panels destroyed, and the marble slabs of the flooring disfigured. The exquisite painted ceilings were used by the fascists as firing targets.

A great deal of work on the part of scholars, architects and restorers was needed to return the palace to its original appearance. The restored Hall was opened to the public in 1958, and from 1961 onwards other rooms have also been opened.

East Pavilion

Today visitors enter Monplaisir through a small pavilion once called the Amusement House. Square in ground plan with a brick floor and four large glass doors, it has a four-faceted dome reminiscent of a tent roof. The facets of the dome were painted by masters from the Armoury from sketches by Philippe Pillement in 1721. At one time the south facade was also decorated with painting, traces of which can still be seen today. The interior is hung with paintings by French, Dutch and Flemish masters of the 17th and early 18th century. Among the Dutch works the most interesting is Adriaan Van der Werff's *Vertumnus and Pomona* depicting the mythological subject of the god of gardens' love for the goddess of fruit. The paintings in the pavilion form part of the large Monplaisir art collection, which contains 147 works acquired on the initiative of Peter the Great or his emissaries. The galleries linking the pavilions with the central section were particularly good for displaying them.

East Gallery

The broad sections of the north wall made it possible to hang pictures here in pairs, one above the other. The entablatures and ceilings of the galleries are adorned with splendid ornamental painting with the use of gold, the work of Philippe Pillement and his Russian assistants. There is an allegorical representation of Summer in the middle of the ceiling.

Today there are twenty-one canvases hanging in the gallery. Two places are still empty. The pictures that hung here were removed long ago in the 18th century, and replacements have not yet been found. For the most part the paintings here are the work of Dutch and Flemish masters of the 17th and 18th centuries. They reflect the tastes of Peter the Great, and were for the most part acquired at auctions in Amsterdam which Peter often visited. Apart from the tsar's special fondness for sea subjects, one cannot detect any other principles in the selection of the works.

The works in the East Gallery contain several pairs: the two trick paintings by an unknown artist, *Engraving of an Old Man* and *Still Life with Medals and Watches,* and the canvases by the Flemish painter Van Heil *The Fall of Sodom* and *Aeneas' Flight From Troy.* The most valuable are *The Departure for the Hunt* by Philips Wouwerman and *A Seascape* by Adriaan Van de Velde.

Lacquered Study

As you cross the threshold of this room you seem to enter the magical world of the Orient. The walls are covered with black lacquered panels in bright red frames. The painting on the black background with relief figures is done in gold. The landscapes, gardens and scenes of hunting and fishing are surrounded by animals, birds, plants and fantastic creatures. There are gilt consoles on the vertical pilaster strips between the panels.

Work on the décor of the study began in 1719 from a design by Johann Braunstein. The lacquer painting was done by Russian icon-painters under the guidance of the Dutch master Hendrik van Bronkhorst. By February 1722 all ninety-four panels were finished and brought to Peterhof from St Petersburg. It is interesting to see that in the hands of the Russian masters the Chinese subjects acquired characteristic Russian features. The fantastic bird traditional in Chinese art became similar to the Russian Fire Bird and the exotic Oriental plants to the wild flowers of Central Russia.

All this magnificence was barbarically destroyed during the war.

When specialists entered the room again in January 1944 they saw nothing but bare brick walls. Craftsmen from the village of

112 Palekh outside Moscow made a splendid job of restoring the panels. With great accuracy they reproduced all the subjects of the original painting from photographs and the few surviving panels (between the windows on the south side of the study). The consoles were remade from small fragments of the original carving.

The ceiling painted by Pillement with an allegorical representation of Autumn in the form of a Bacchante with a bunch of grapes and a cup of wine, was more fortunate. Both the painting and the exquisite moulded frame survived and had only to be restored.

On the consoles in the study are various items of Chinese work that have been in Monplaisir since Peter's day. They testify to the trading links that existed since early times between Russia and the Far East.

Ceremonial Hall

A door from the Lacquered Study leads to the central room of the palace, the Ceremonial Hall. Its glass doors face south and north, i.e., the garden and the sea. The ceremonial nature of the hall is emphasised by its dimensions and rich décor. It was used for diplomatic receptions and balls. As in the galleries, the walls are adorned with paintings in black lacquered frames.

Take a good look at the painting on the dome-shaped ceiling by Philippe Pillement. The four facets of the entablature have compositions symbolising the four elements in the form of Greek gods: Water (as Neptune, god of the sea), Air (as Juno, the goddess of marriage), Fire (as Vulcan, the god of fire) and Earth (as Flora, the goddess of flowers and spring).

Higher up framed by moulded drapings are allegorical representations of the four winds and four temperaments, and over it all reigns Apollo, the god of sun and patron of the arts.

The artist is speaking in the language of symbols about the constant change in the world, the rotation of the seasons, the swift passage of time. Only art stands above real life. Art is eternal, immortal.

Of the twenty-two paintings in the Hall by Dutch and Flemish masters the most interesting are the ships at sea by Adam Silo. There are five of his paintings in Monplaisir. As an artist he did not stand out particularly from the other Dutch masters of his day. But he was able to paint ships and all their parts with remarkable accuracy, as he was also a shipbuilder, glass-polisher, ship's captain and engraver. It was this diversity that endeared him to Peter the Great when the Russian tsar was studying ship-building in Amsterdam. Peter is said to have used his painting to examine pupils at the Russian Naval Academy founded in 1715.

Kitchen

The central door in the east wall of the Ceremonial Hall leads to the Kitchen. Its décor was finished in the summer of 1723. The somewhat unusual proximity of a room with a purely utilitarian function to a ceremonial chamber is usually explained by the fact that, as Peter's contemporaries reported, "His Majesty ate little and ordered that the food should be hot, and that the kitchen should be in the palace next to his dining room." Banquets for visitors to Monplaisir were not prepared in here, but in some other rooms. The main reason, however, was that in Dutch houses of which Peter was so fond this arrangement was customary.

In the Dutch manner the palace kitchen has a large hearth with a cowl and wall shelves, and its walls are tiled from top to bottom. The blue of the tiles gives the room a special flavour and creates an impression of cleanliness and tidiness. These tiles were brought to Russia from the Dutch town of Delft. Russian masters soon learnt to make them. There are fifty different subjects on the tiles in the kitchen: landscapes with houses and animals, figures of people, ships sailing in the sea, and so on.

The Nazis destroyed all the tiles, but Soviet experts succeeded in reproducing the artistic style of the old masters very accurately.

The numerous English pewter items, the Russian copper articles, Delft china and Chinese porcelain are in keeping with the room's function.

Pantry

The table ware and table linen were stored here. This is the only room in the palace in which the walls have no ornament. They are simply plastered and nothing more. It cannot be said that the pantry is completely void of décor, however. It has an interesting parquet floor, a moulded fireplace, and a splendid painting on the ceiling by Philippe Pillement of Winter in the form of a woman with a brazier.

Appropriately enough the Pantry contains glass and ceramic dinner services: Delft dishes and vases, Russian glass decanters and all manner of goblets and glasses. On the fireplace are eight teapots made of brown clay, which are said to be a present to Peter the Great from the Emperor of China.

Marine Study

Of the Emperor's private apartments that adjoin the Ceremonial Hall to the west the most interesting is his Study. Its three windows face the sea. Through the lattice windows he could see Kronstadt in one direction and St Petersburg in the other. Peter was very fond of this room, rightly called the Marine Study. If you raised the lower half of the window slightly, you could take a spy-glass and watch the vessels sailing to and from the northern capital.

The walls were faced with oak and inlaid with tiles showing thirteen different types of ships of the early 18th century. On the ceiling

Pillement painted monkeys frisking about in an oval frame. The pictures here are also interesting: eleven landscapes by the Austrian Franz de Paula Ferg, three works on Greek subjects by the Flemish painter Victor Janssens and some others.

Bedroom

After the Study comes the Bedroom. In the centre is a huge four-poster bed with curtains. It is a copy. The original is in the House of Peter the Great Museum in Tallinn. There are several of Peter's personal possessions here. On the bed lie his dressing gown and night-cap. The wash-stand was made in the 17th century in the Spanish town of Pamplona. The wooden mug with three glasses and a salt-cellar on the wash-stand were made and painted by Archangel craftsmen. Here too are a black lacquered wash-jug and basin of English make.

The walls are hung with green fabric. The ceiling is painted with traditional characters from Italian commedia dell'arte. The fine plastic moulding of the fireplace adds a special elegance to the interior. The military trophies and the Order of St Andrew (the highest in the Russian Empire) represented here are somewhat out of place in the intimate atmosphere of the bedroom.

Secretary's Room

This room, which adjoins the bedroom to the south, belonged to the Emperor's personal secretary. In terms of décor, however, it was no different from the Emperor's private apartments: oak-panelled walls, parquet flooring, a moulded fireplace, and a ceiling painted with Bacchic scenes. What is more, in the quantity and quality of its paintings the Secretary's Room is even richer than Peter's Study. It contains twenty-four pictures. Of these the most interesting are two

116 paintings by Adriaan Van der Salm painted on wood in grisaille (a
style of painting that uses two tints of one colour, usually grey or
brown) and showing the harbours of Archangel and Amsterdam,
evidence of the long-standing connection between these ports, a
painting by Alessandro Grevenbroeck depicting *A Naval Battle
Between Russian Galleys and the Swedish Fleet* showing the battle
of Hängo (1714) and Jan Wynants' *Landscape with a Herd,* the
figures of which were painted by another Dutch master, Adriaan
Van de Velde. During the war all the paintings in the Secretary's
Room were evacuated and thus escaped destruction. When restoration work on this room was completed, the pictures were rehung
using red cord in exactly the same order they had during Peter the
Great's reign.

West Gallery and Pavilion

Architecturally they are identical to the corresponding gallery
and pavilion on the east side of the palace. Here as there the decisive
role in the interior décor is played by painting. The ceiling of the
gallery is painted with grotesque ornament. The medallions contain
the figure of the goddess Flora, a symbol of spring, and the figure of
a youth with a tambourine shown in one against the rising sun and
in another against the setting sun.

The composition and nature of the pictures in the West Gallery
and Pavilion and their subjects are more or less the same as in the
other rooms of the palace. Here too we find works by Adam Silo and
Dutch and Flemish masters of which the most interesting is the seascape by Willem Van de Velde, fils, and two views of the Dutch town
of Saardam (Zandam), where Peter lived and worked incognito in
1697. These two paintings are the work of Franz van der Horn.

One of Peter's drawings relating to the construction of Peterhof shows a plan for a small garden on the seashore by Monplaisir palace. There are also instructions written in the Emperor's hand as to what plants should be put in the flower-beds and in what order. Another drawing sketches the avenues round the perimeter of the future garden. Work on the garden was completed in 1718. It contained limes, chestnuts and maple trees, and some trellises.

In August 1721 under Peter's direct supervision work commenced on building the fountains, which began to play in 1723. The focal point of the whole composition was the Wheatsheaf Fountain in the centre of the garden. A powerful jet of water shoots up from a high pedestal surrounded by two tiers of vertical jets that resemble a sheaf of wheat. The water falls into a basin with five cascades of white marble.

The other four fountains in the garden work on the same principle and are called the Bells. They are on either side of the Wheatsheaf and were designed by Niccolo Michetti. Initially they were adorned with gilded lead figures which were copies of the Greek sculptures of young Apollo and Ganymede and of Renaissance sculptures by Giovanni Rosso (Faun) and Jacopo Sansovino (Bacchus). In 1817 new bronze figures of Apollo, the Faun and Bacchus were cast from models by Ivan Martos. Ganymede was replaced by Antonio Canova's Psyche. Rising from apertures under the circular bases of the statues, the water forms transparent bells, which explains the fountains' name.

Note the two modest white seats with gilded mascarons on their backs. These are the jester fountains. At one time trellised arcades led to them from the Monplaisir pavilions. Flushed with merrymaking, the ladies and their partners would come out to get a breath of fresh sea air. They would see the seats tucked away in the garden and hurry up to them suspecting nothing. Suddenly out of nowhere

118 thin jets of water shot out soaking them from head to foot. The air still rings with the laughter and exclamations of visitors caught unawares today.

STEAM BATHS AND BATHING POOLS

Among its domestic buildings Monplaisir had bathing pools and steam baths. These buildings were first made of wood. In 1800 the Steam Baths were rebuilt in stone from a design by Giacomo Quarenghi that linked them architecturally with the existing buildings. As well as a steam room and ordinary baths there was a Ladies-in-Waiting Pool, an octagonal basin with a pipe running round the edge that had jets of water spurting from the many apertures.

The Bathing Pools erected in 1748 is a most interesting building. It first contained crystal baths in a copper casing. But in 1769 a pool was built for Catherine II with a sliding panel at the bottom that let in sea-water. A complex mechanism made it possible to regulate the water level. Fresh water was supplied from the figure in the centre of the pool, which was later replaced by a column bearing a globe.

During the rebuilding of the Bathing Pools in 1865—1866 the Empress's pool was preserved and survived until 1941.

ASSEMBLY HALL

In 1747 Bartholomeo Rastrelli was instructed to turn the Kitchen Hall into an Assembly Hall "for cavaliers to dine in". It was hung with seventeen tapestries made in the second quarter of the 18th century at the St Petersburg Tapestry Manufactory. Eight of them were replicas of a well-known series of Indian Gobelins by François Desportes.

In 1755 an adjoining kitchen was built on with a *Tafeldecker* in which the china and table linen were kept and a room where coffee, tea and other beverages were prepared.

All the tapestries of the Assembly Hall have survived and will be rehung in their former places when restoration work has been completed.

CHINESE GARDEN

This garden was laid out in 1865-1866 from a design by the architect Edward Hahn, when the Bathing Pools were being rebuilt. A small artificial hill was built and a channel for a stream with two hump-backed wooden bridges. The water in the stream comes from the Shell Fountain, behind which in the shrubs are the white marble statues of Cupid and Psyche, an early 19th-century copy of the Greek original. By the blank wall of the kitchen is an 18th-century statue of Mercury and a fountain by the east entrance to the Bathing Pools. In a small circular basin from a pink marble vase made in 1805 and designed by Andrei Voronikhin for the Hermitage Cascade a vertical jet rises and interplays with a similar jet in the small lake into which the stream flows.

CATHERINE PALACE

In the early period of Monplaisir's existence there was a kitchen garden opposite the Steam Baths and other domestic outbuildings on the western edge of the park. Later a small stone conservatory was built there. In 1748 Rastrelli used its foundations to build a stone palace for the Empress Elizabeth that was larger than Monplaisir, making it possible to hold receptions, balls and other entertainments there. The palace also had residential quarters in wooden galleries. The original décor did not survive for long. In the 1780s Giacomo Quarenghi redecorated all the state rooms.

The Green Reception Room, Yellow Hall, Blue Drawing Room, and Front and Corner Drawing Rooms have windows facing east and south; while the Heating Room, and Alexander I's Bedchamber and Study face west. The private rooms of Catherine the Great survived in the wooden galleries right up to 1941. She lived in them even before she ascended the throne. It was from here on 28 June, 1762 accompanied by the Guards Officer Alexei Orlov, that she left for St Petersburg to depose her husband Peter III with the help of regiments loyal to her. In memory of her period of residence here the palace was named after her.

The wooden galleries were burnt down in the war, and the stone building was destroyed at the same time. The palace collections were evacuated.

When restoration work is completed they will be returned to their former places in the Catherine Palace.

MONPLAISIR AVENUE

This straight avenue runs from Monplaisir Garden to the Chess Hill Cascade (described below). The entrance to it from the south is flanked by 18th-century replicas of Apollo and Mercury.

At the intersection with Marly Avenue are four marble female busts, Italian work of the first half of the 18th century. In the middle of the intersection is a statue of Peter the Great designed by Mark Antokolsky in 1883 standing on a pedestal designed by Edward Hahn in 1884. During the occupation of Peterhof the Nazis stole the statue. A new one was cast in 1956 from the original model in the Russian Museum.

MENAGERIE

A permanent feature of many formal gardens in the early 18th century was the menagerie with exotic animals and birds. Peter the Great included one in the Monplaisir ensemble. Peacocks, turkeys and storks strutted about in it.

A large pond was built for water-fowl in 1718-1719. But only two years later a fountain was erected in it, and another pond was dug a little to the east of it, which became known as the Swan Pond. At the same time construction began of two elegant wooden pavilions designed by Niccolo Michetti. They were completed by 1722. Cages of singing birds and parrots were installed in them.

Each pavilion had a central octagonal edifice with a domed roof. To the right and left were two small rooms. The walls and dome were painted by Louis Caravacque with ornament and figures from Greek mythology.

The menagerie survived during the occupation and was partially restored in 1959.

SUN FOUNTAIN

Not far from the west menagerie is a pond with brick walls. During Peter's day it contained some huge sturgeon, as well as ducks, geese and swans. In 1721-1729 Michetti built a fountain here. Later after some alterations it was decided to build a bathing pool on this spot. This work was carried out in 1774-1776 by Yuri Velten.

The appearance of the basin and the fountain were changed somewhat. In the centre a tall socle was erected containing a wheel turned by the water which caused a column surrounded by sixteen dolphins to revolve. On top of the column were two parallel disks with numerous holes in their edges. The jets of water shooting out of these holes resembled the rays of the sun. The fountain was destroyed by the Nazis, but restored in 1957. The restorers preserved its original mechanism.

Near the Sun Fountain is a group of marble sculptures. Three of them, the Bacchus and two Bacchantes, are 18th-century and *Psyche with a Butterfly* (1830s) is a replica of the work by Antonio Canova. The two pairs of *Cupids Riding on Dolphins* on the edge of the basin were made in 1848.

These occupy a special place among the 18th-century Peterhof fountains. Nowhere else in the world can you find so many trick fountains as in the Petrodvorets parks, although at one time they were almost a compulsory feature of the formal garden. As well as the seat in Monplaisir, the trick fountains known as the Little Oak, the Fir Tree and the Umbrella are still working.

Walking round the park at the height of summer visitors suddenly see some beautiful tulips under a shady "oak tree". They bend down to take a closer look, and jets of water suddenly shoot up at them from the flowers. They step back hurriedly under the oak tree, only to be greeted by further jets from the leaves and branches, which are made of hollow pipes. The visitors flee to two welcoming benches nearby, but jets of water shoot up from them too inscribing an arc, that gives them yet another soaking.

The Little Oak fountain was erected in 1735 in one of the basins of the Upper Park, then taken down and stored away from the middle of the 18th to the beginning of the 19th century. In 1802 it was erected in its present place.

Near the Little Oak are three "Fir Trees". Their "branches", skilfully made of pipes, send forth silvery jets like continuations of the green needles. This fountain was made in 1784 by Fyodor Strelnikov, who later became one of the finest fountain-makers in Peterhof.

At the intersection of Monplaisir Avenue and Marly Avenue is a small column with an umbrella-shaped roof and a circular seat round its base. Along the edge of the roof is a hidden pipe with 164 apertures. As soon as anyone sits on the seat, the fountain begins to work. It is almost impossible to get away without being soaked. The Umbrella Fountain was made in 1796 from a design by the architect Franz Brouer.

All these unusual fountains have been through hard times. The

Little Oak was dismantled in 1914 and stored away in the museum for ten years until it was found by restorers in 1924, repaired and erected in the Lower Park. The Fir Trees were also removed in the second half of the 19th century and not put back until 1938.

During the occupation the Nazis destroyed the trick fountains. A few details miraculously survived (a branch and some leaves from the Little Oak) and from these and odd information in the archives specialists managed to restore the fountains.

ROMAN FOUNTAINS

These fountains make up a two-tiered composition. A marble bowl with curved sides rests on a huge, cubic pedestal. On top of it is a smaller cube, also with a bowl from the centre of which five jets play, forming a pyramid. The water falls onto the edge of the bowls and from there into basins of intricate Baroque design.

The fountains were built in 1738-1739 from a design by the architects Karl Blank and Ivan Davydov. They were very like the fountains in front of St Peter's in Rome. Hence their name. In 1797-1800 they were rebuilt to a design produced earlier by Rastrelli.

The ornament of the Roman Fountains includes various types of coloured marble, decorated garlands, wreaths and mascarons cast from a model by Ivan Martos in 1817.

CHESS HILL
(DRAGON CASCADE)

At the end of Monplaisir Avenue is the Chess Hill Cascade—four huge sloping steps painted in a black and white zigzag pattern. At the foot and top of the cascade are grottos. The entrance to the upper grotto is guarded by three dragons from whose open jaws powerful jets of water shoot up and fall down the steps.

Chess Hill Cascade

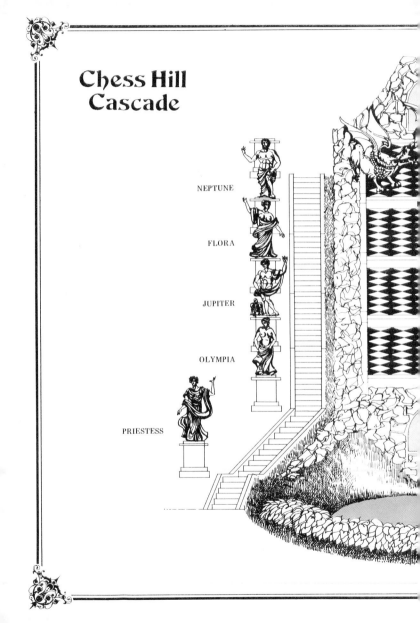

NEPTUNE

FLORA

JUPITER

OLYMPIA

PRIESTESS

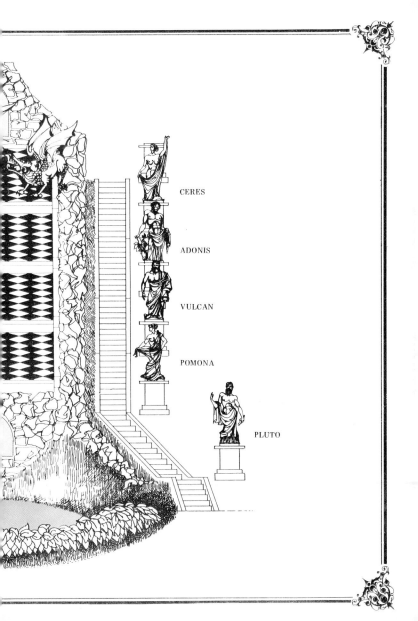

CERES

ADONIS

VULCAN

POMONA

PLUTO

126 Right and left along the wooden balustrades are ten marble statues of mythological figures by 18th-century Italian sculptors.

The cascade was built in 1739 from a design by Mikhail Zemtsov. At first it was called Dragon Hill. It acquired its present name in the middle of the 18th century when its steps were painted in a chequered pattern.

When the Nazis were approaching Leningrad, the cascade's marble statues were buried in the Lower Park. After the liberation of Peterhof they were dug up and put in place again. And in 1953 some dragons made by the sculptor Alexei Gurzhy from an 18th-century drawing appeared on the restored cascade.

PYRAMID FOUNTAIN

This fountain is particularly striking for its many jets and interesting pattern. It stands on one of the avenues leading north-east from the Roman Fountains.

During a visit to France in 1717 Peter was particularly impressed at Versailles by a fountain in the form of a three-sided obelisk made up of water jets.

After his victory in the Northern War the Emperor continued to embellish his beloved Peterhof and remembered the Versailles water obelisk. In 1721 he instructed Michetti to make a replica of this fountain, but one in the form of a pyramid. "I saw that the one in France had about five hundred jets," he told the architect. Three years later another new fountain appeared in the Lower Park. The pyramid was formed by 505 jets rising to various heights. The water fell into a square basin from which it flowed down four cascades facing the points of the compass into a canal.

During the war the Pyramid Fountain was destroyed. It was restored in 1953.

Hermitage Pavilion

In the west section of the Lower Park, tucked away along an oblique avenue that runs from the Grand Flower-beds, stands an elegant two-storey building on the sea-shore. Above the entrance is a balcony supported by carved oak corbels. The balcony has wrought-iron railings. The walls are adorned with pilasters with Corinthian capitals and high pedestals. The high glass doors and windows with their magnificent views give the building a special airiness. Its name describes the purpose of the building that was cut off from the inquisitive by a deep moat. Only a drawbridge, that could be lowered or pulled up as the inhabitants of the pavilion wished, linked them with the outside world.

Peter the Great decided to build the Hermitage Pavilion on his return from a visit to Europe where this type of pavilion was in fashion. Its construction, from a design by Johann Braunstein, took a long time and it was not completed until after the Emperor's death, in the summer of 1725. Everything here was done as Peter had planned it: the lifting mechanisms and the wrought-iron railings on the balconies as on his flagship, the *Ingermanlandia*, aboard which Peter had commanded the joint fleets of Russia, Britain, and Holland in the Northern War, a table for fourteen people, and a great deal more.

The Hermitage Pavilion suffered greatly during World War II. The Nazis set up a cannon on the first floor to bombard the Gulf of Finland. As a result part of the wall and the balconies were destroyed.

128   In 1952 the Hermitage again opened its doors to the public. It was the first museum in Petrodvorets to be restored. In 1970-1971 extensive work was carried out to reinforce the base and restore the facing of the moat walls. This made it possible to preserve the pavilion without rebuilding its walls.

The entrance leads to a narrow vestibule beyond which is the large Pantry. It was here that the table was set: through an oval opening in the ceiling with the help of two winches the central part of the table in the Hall on the first floor was lowered along vertical beams to the ground floor; when it had been set with the requisite cutlery, dishes, etc., it was hauled up again and disappeared through the opening in the ceiling. There was a kitchen with a hearth and spare utensils on the ground floor to the right of the Pantry.

To the left of the Pantry is a staircase leading to the first floor. In the 18th century its place was taken by what might be regarded as the first Russian lift, a kind of lift-chair for two people. It worked right up to the end of the 18th century. In June 1797 Emperor Paul I and his family decided to visit the Hermitage. As the Emperor was going up in the lift-chair, the mechanism suddenly jammed and the chair with its august passengers was left swinging between the two floors. They had to be rescued with the help of a ladder placed against the balcony. Orders were given for the mechanism to be removed and the present stairs to be built.

The whole of the first floor is taken up by one very light and airy room, the reason why the whole building was erected. The high ceiling, the glass doors and windows on all four sides, and the pictures covering the walls give the room an impressive, dignified air. Originally it was intended for retiring with an intimate circle of friends of similar status and interests. Nothing and no one was to intrude on the privacy of those assembled here.

Fourteen people sat at the large oval table. Each had a place set for him. The central part of the table, as already mentioned, was hauled up from the ground floor with the dishes on it. Yet each of the guests, if he so wished, could order a dish just for himself. All he had to do was write down his request on a piece of paper, put it on a plate and pull a cord. A bell then rang downstairs in the Pantry, and the servants lowered the plate down a special chute. Then the plate was sent up with the order which appeared before the guest as if by magic.

The table was destroyed by the Nazis during the war. A replica of it stands in the hall today. But the services and table linen are exactly the same as they were in the 18th century: the china with the cobalt design was made in Delft in 1750-1760 and the numerous glasses, goblets and decanters were mostly made at the Imperial manufactory in the 18th century.

The Hall's main decoration is 124 pictures by West European and Russian artists. This tapestry of paintings first appeared here in 1759. The pictures now hanging here, most of which belong to the collection as it was restored after a fire in 1809, give a clear idea of the styles of painting and artistic tastes in the 17th and 18th centuries.

On the spot once taken up by the tambour of the lift-chair hangs the *Battle of Poltava*. Commissioned by Peter the Great in France in 1726 from Pierre Martin and reproduced in a gobelin and numerous engravings, this picture was frequently copied in Russia. The copy now in the Hermitage is the work of an unknown 18th-century Russian artist.

Also on the west wall is a canvas by the highly popular 17th-century painter of battle scenes Jacques Courtois. Next to it are still lifes by the Frenchman Jean Louis Prevost, the scene *Ice Skating* by the Flemish master Louis Chalon, and others. There is no definite theme or system in the arrangement of the pictures. In some cases, however, a certain symmetry is observed. In the lower right-hand corner of the west wall are two smallish paintings of the apostles, the work of the Dutch painter Georg Gsell, who was invited to Russia by Peter the Great and lived there for twenty-three years. Two

130 similar works by the same painter are hanging on the north wall.

Other works of interest on the north wall are Giovanni Battista Langetti's *Death of Cato,* depicting the suicide of this tribune of the people in Ancient Rome who refused to submit to the dictatorship of Caesar; *Anthony and Cleopatra* by the Flemish painter Gerard de Lairesse and *The Temptation of St Anthony* by the Flemish master Abraham Teniers.

The most valuable of the paintings on the east wall are the splendid bunch of flowers by the Flemish artist Gaspar Pieter Verbruggen and the Italian works of *Apollo and Marsyas* by Giulio Carpioni and *Antiochus and Stratonica* by Gaspare Diziani. The latter tells of the love of Antiochus, son of King Seleuctus of Syria, for his stepmother Stratonica.

The south wall is hung with a whole series of battle scenes by Jacques Courtois, the German painter Georg Philipp Rugendas and the Italian Michelangelo Cerquozzi alongside idyllic landscapes, genre scenes and portraits by Austrian, Dutch and Flemish masters.

The small but rich and varied collection of the Hermitage enables us not only to see the world through the eyes of masters of the 17th and 18th centuries, but also to form an idea of how paintings were collected and exhibited in 18th-century Russia.

LION CASCADE

This cascade, which is compositionally linked with the Hermitage, did not appear in the Lower Park until 1799-1800. Moreover the architect Andrei Voronikhin placed it not on the slope, but in the square between the Birch Tree and Marly avenues. On a low stone wall stood eight vases and the figures of Hercules and Flora, replaced a year later by two lions. The water from the vases fell into a rectangular upper basin, then down two steps into the lower basin.

In 1854-55 the architect Andrei Stakenschneider reconstructed Voronikhin's fountain. On a granite socle, identical in ground plan to the old cascade, he set up a colonnade of fourteen eight-metre high Ionic columns. They were made of dark grey granite and their bases and capitals were of white Carrara marble. By the colonnade stood bronze lions with jets gushing out of their jaws. On a granite mound in the middle of the basin, which was surrounded on three sides by the colonnade, stood the graceful figure of the nymph Aganippa, the work of the sculptor Fyodor Tolstoy.

During the war part of the colonnade was destroyed and the Nazis stole all the sculpture. Work is at present in progress to restore this fountain, the largest to be built in Russia in the 19th century.

Château de Marly

Almost at the western edge of the Lower Park, between two ponds, stands a two-storey palace painted yellow ochre. In spite of its relatively small proportions it plays an important role in the layout of the whole Lower Park. From it the park's three main avenues fan out, the Central Marly, the North Maliban and the South Birch Tree Avenue. The palace is also the architectural centre of the ensemble containing two parks, a cascade and fountains.

In 1720 Johann Braunstein produced a design for a small single-storey building between ponds near the seashore. A year later it was completed. Peter found it somewhat unimpressive, however, and ordered a second floor to be added. In 1723 the palace was ready. It was named after the French kings' residence at Marly-de-Roi near Paris. True, the Peterhof Marly could in no way rival the huge palace ensemble in France.

The Château de Marly has seven rooms on each floor with an identical layout. The floors are linked by a staircase with a splendid wrought-iron balustrade with gilded details.

Entering the château from the pond side the visitor finds himself in a corridor leading into the Hall. The corridors of both floors are hung with paintings. On the ground floor, for example, we find Gerard Seghers' *Antiquarian Shop,* a canvas by an unknown 18th-century Dutch painter entitled *The Leaning Towers of Bologna* and *A Philosopher* by a painter of the Rembrandt school.

Kitchen

As in Monplaisir, the interior of the Marly kitchen reminds one of a typical Dutch kitchen: the marble-tiled floor, the huge stove under a hood in the corner, the walls covered with ceramic tiles from top to bottom. The Marly tiles are richer than those in the Monplaisir kitchen.

There is kitchenware on the shelves, tables and stove: English and German pewter, copper pots and pans from the Urals, and Dutch and German ceramics.

The grandfather clock hanging between the windows was made in the 18th century in Ostfriesland (North Germany).

Pantry

This is where the tableware and table linen was kept. The furniture in this room, the sideboard, cabinet, wash-stand and chairs, are typical of such rooms in the 18th century. The walls are hung with mid-17th century Chinese plates, and 18th-century dishes by German and Dutch craftsmen (Frankfurt-am-Main and Delft). The shelves of the dresser have Chinese and Japanese plates and Russian glass.

Front Hall

This is the most spacious room on the ground floor. Of special interest here are the paintings, part of Marly's extremely interesting collection now consisting of forty-five pictures almost all of which formed part of the décor in the Petrine period.

On the west wall are two huge canvases of *Christ Preaching in*

134 *the Temple* by Andrea Celesti and *Christ and the Adulteress* by
Tiziano Vecellio, Titian's grand nephew.

The two 18th-century glass cabinets of Dutch work contain some
specimens of Canton enamel and a small collection of silver. The
grandfather clock was made by Willem Coster in Amsterdam in the
first third of the 18th century. A copper chandelier (1737) hangs
from the ceiling.

Secretary Room

The room on the south-east corner of the palace, between the
Bedchamber and the Front Hall, was for the secretary on duty. Its
frieze is decorated with elegant moulded bas-reliefs of two types
representing war trophies. The furniture is extremely simple: a table,
a chair, a cupboard and a trunk. The south wall is hung with a
Flemish tapestry of the late 16th century.

Château de Marly

Ground floor

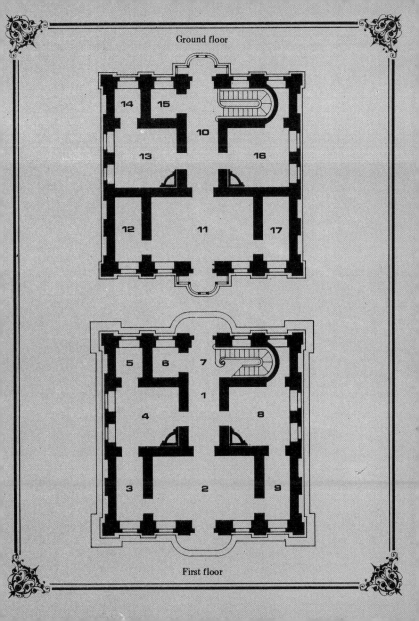

First floor

Bedchamber

As in the other Peterhof palaces built in Peter's day, the walls in the Marly are hung with silk and the bed has a heavy canopy. The inlaid furniture is the work of German masters. Between the windows on a table are Peter the Great's washing utensils, a jug, basin, and soap-dish, all made of painted and lacquered papier mâché. On the bed are Peter's blanket and dressing-gown of embroidered Chinese silk, and his towel.

FIRST FLOOR
Wardrobe Room

The Château de Marly was once the main storing place for Peter the Great's wardrobe. In 1848 most of the Emperor's wardrobe was presented to the Hermitage Museum. But the items on display in the palace are also precious relics of the Petrine age.

Here you can see his naval great-coat, his kaftan embroidered with the Order of St Andrew, his cap and other objects.

Drawing Room

Of the forty-five pictures in the Marly collection, seven belong to the brush of Alessandro Grevenbroeck. The interest in this artist is explained first and foremost by the genre in which he worked. His pale blue seascapes, exotic harbours and fortresses illumined by the golden rays of the sun captivated Peter, who loved the sea. Four of Grevenbroeck's canvases are on display in this room.

Corner Room

This room did not serve a definite purpose nor have any permanent furnishings. Today it contains an ebony pearl-incrusted cabinet made in Germany and some leather upholstered Portuguese chairs. Of the three porcelain vases the most interesting is the middle one with a painting of St Martin covering a beggar with his cloak (1746).

Dressing Room

The six oak chairs upholstered with tapestry are among the few items of furniture that were saved from destruction in 1941. It is thought that these tapestries were manufactured in St Petersburg at the Tapestry Works founded in 1716.

The painting *Ships at Sea* on the east wall is the work of Adam Silo.

Dining Room

In spite of the low ceiling this room gives an impression of space. This is largely due to the abundance of light from the two windows and glass balcony doors. There is a splendid view of the pond, the terraces and the three avenues fanning out into the park. The paintings of fantastic architecture by Italian masters also enhance the impression of spaciousness.

The huge 17th-century English table in the middle is a reminder of the room's original function. The Emperor used to dine here with a few of his closest friends.

Library

In Peter's day the Marly library was a small one with only a few score books, but the fact that a special room was set aside for it testifies to the changes that were taking place in the life of the Russian aristocracy. The Marly collection of books has changed somewhat over the years and only a few of those in the original collection remain today. But in general the library, which survived the war, gives one a good idea of 18th-century private book collections.

Oak Study

In the north-east corner of the first floor is a small study with oak-lined walls. The oak panels and strips are decorated with some sparse but elegant carving from designs by Nicolas Pineau. By the window on a desk reputed to have been made by Peter himself is an intricate bronze sun-dial, a present from King William I to the Russian Emperor during a visit by Peter to England.

For more than a century and a half the Marly remained unaltered. But at the end of the 19th century cracks appeared in the walls. After careful measurement and removal of some of the interior décor the château was dismantled down to the foundations, and after the foundations had been reinforced, put together again from the same materials.

As they were retreating in 1944 the Nazis blew up the palace. It was restored in 1982.

GOLDEN HILL CASCADE

This cascade is the architectural focal point of the western part of the Lower Park. The white marble steps, the gold leaf of their verticals, the splendid collection of sculpture, and the stone staircases with balustrades all make it unusually striking. At the foot is a gigantic jet of water, and around the cascade four gilded tritons gleam through the veil of water.

In the year that the château was built Peter commissioned Niccolo Michetti to design a cascade. The edifice was completed at the same time as the palace, in 1723. In 1731-1732 the architect Mikhail Zemtsov reconstructed the cascade. On the side walls at the bottom and on the small wall at the top he erected five figures of marble and two of gilded bronze, as well as mascarons of the

Medusa. He edged the verticals of the steps with gilded bronze plates that produce an interesting interplay of light through the mirror of the cascading water. Ever since then the cascade has been called the Golden Hill.

The completion of the sculptural ornament (1869-1870) is associated with the architect Nikolai Benois. It was on his initiative that ten marble figures of Greek gods were acquired to replace the lead sculpture. Then, too, the steps were faced with white marble.

During the war the cascade was badly damaged. All the sculpture, with the exception of the *Faun with a Goat* in the lower basin, was saved, however, and returned to its original place after restoration. The *Faun* was replaced by a mid-18th-century sculpture of *Spring*.

MENAGERNY FOUNTAINS

The name of these fountains, which form a compositional entity with the Golden Hill, did not appear until the middle of the 19th century. The principle on which they work and their technical construction date back to 1722-1724, however. They were built from sketches and a plan thought up by Peter. Their name comes from the French verb *menager* meaning "to economise". These huge jets of up to fifteen metres produce an impression of an incredible amount of water. In fact they are hollow. The apertures of the jets are pipes thirty centimeters in diameter. Inside them are cones facing downwards. Between the cones and the walls of the pipes there is a half-a-centimetre gap all round through which the hollow column of water spurts with great force, a most economical use of water indeed.

TRITON FOUNTAINS

In 1724 on the northern limit of the parterre it was proposed to build four fountains illustrating Aesop's fables. A few years later,

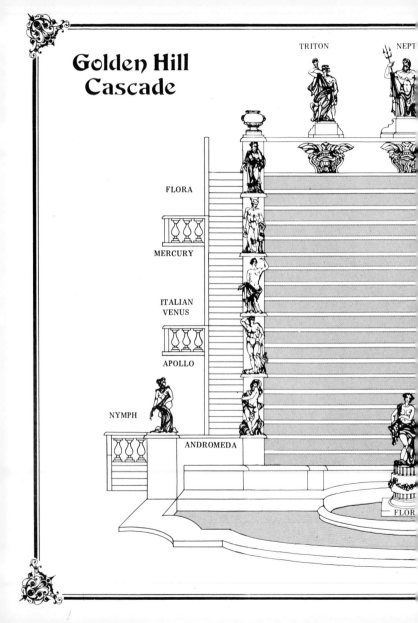

Golden Hill Cascade

TRITON

NEPT

FLORA

MERCURY

ITALIAN
VENUS

APOLLO

NYMPH

ANDROMEDA

FLOR

BACCHUS

MINERVA

VULCAN

MEDICI
VENUS

FAUN

NEPTUNE

FLORA

142   however, it was decided to erect here the lead figures of four young tritons cast in England in 1721. Above their heads they were supporting wooden craters faced with lead. Each crater had four jets.

At the end of the 18th century the craters were replaced by flat discs through the centre of which ran pipes with circular pieces of metal covering the nozzle. The water spurting out of the pipes hits the pieces of metal and falls down, forming bell-like shapes. This explains the second name by which the fountains are known, the *Cloches,* which is French for "bells".

The Nazis destroyed the sculpture of the fountains. In 1954 the Tritons were restored from a model by Alexei Gurzhy.

Alexandria
Park

❦

To the east of the Lower Park on the shore of the Gulf of Finland lies the Alexandria Park covering an area of 115 hectares. Here too the terraced layout is preserved. But this park is quite different. There are clusters of oak trees, maples, limes and other trees dotted about the large open meadows. Small paths wind over the terraces and green lawns and a brook babbles in a gully spanned by a "ruined bridge". The romantic atmosphere of the park is enhanced by small buildings in Gothic style.

Alexandria was conceived and constructed in the second half of the 19th century as an Imperial summer residence, the private possession of the Romanov family. In August 1825 Emperor Alexander I presented this land to his brother Nicholas, who was crowned Emperor four months later and made a present of it to his wife Alexandra, after whom the estate is named.

Building here began in 1826 with the Cottage, a palace built in the neo-Gothic style characterised by the use of Gothic architectural features without any organic link between function and construction. In 1829 the architect Adam Menelaws completed work on its décor. This compact, three-storey building, almost square in ground plan, has a roof with steep gables painted the colour of thatch, yet another reminder of its purpose as a country villa. The wrought-iron lattice work of the balconies, the bay windows and terraces, the window grilles, and the moulding of the cornices are all done in the English style of Tudor Gothic. The deep loggias of the east and west façades are also in this style. The details of the décor are painted white to contrast with the ochre of the walls. The coloured glass in the casements of the arcades on the ground floor is also reminiscent of Gothic. Some very fine flower-beds were laid out around the Cottage and the other buildings in the park.

In 1842 the architect Andrei Stakenschneider added a dining room, pantry and marble terrace with a fountain to the Cottage, which had become somewhat cramped for the royal family. This upset the strict symmetry of Menelaws' building, but made it look more homely and attractive.

In 1829-1831 Menelaws built the Farm to the west of the Cottage. This pavilion was intended to impart an air of rural idyll to the park. The Farm was later turned into a palace for Nicholas I's son, Alexander, when he was still heir to the throne (in 1836), and in 1858, three years after he was crowned Emperor of Russia, Stakenschneider gave the Farm its present dimensions.

At the request of Nicholas I the German architect Karl Friedrich Schinkel designed a Gothic church (Capella) for the Alexandria Park in 1829. In 1831-1833 the church was built in the western section of the park on the edge of the upper terrace (architects Adam Menelaws and Ludwig Charlemagne). At different times groups of domestic outbuildings, pavilions, towers, a latticed well and summer-house, guardrooms, etc., were erected.

After the victory of the October Socialist Revolution in accordance with a decree signed by V. I. Lenin, the Alexandria Park and all its palaces privately owned by the Romanovs were declared state property. The Cottage and the other buildings in the park were turned into museums that give a very clear idea of Russian art from the 1820s to the early 20th century.

The Nazis destroyed, damaged and looted the park's fine buildings. Restoration work began when the war ended. The Cottage Palace was the first to be restored. Today work is being carried out to reconstruct the Farm Palace and the domestic buildings.

Cottage Palace

The main entrance to the palace is on the south side of the building. It has an impressive porch with a vaulted arcade.

Vestibule

This is square in ground plan and painted mock marble. On the left hangs a shield made from the shell of a giant marine tortoise. It bears the coat-of-arms of Alexandria, a drawn sword hung with a wreath of roses on a blue background and the inscription: "For Faith, the Tsar and the Fatherland". The author of this heraldic sign was the famous Russian poet Vasily Zhukovsky.

The fascination which the attributes of chivalry held for the owners of the Cottage can also be seen from the stone in the wall over the main door. This stone is from the Turkish fortress of Varna, captured by Russian troops during the Russo-Turkish War of 1828-1829. Just as knights returning from the wars would present their ladies with trophies, so Nicholas I ordered this stone to be set in the Cottage, the palace of his wife Alexandra.

Bedchamber

From the vestibule we turn left through a small room for gentlemen-in-waiting into a large chamber with two windows and a glass door leading onto a balcony on the south facade. This was formerly the Bedchamber. Its ceiling is adorned with lacy Gothic moulding designed by Adam Menelaws and executed by Matvei

Sokolov. Exquisitely modelled and traced with great mastery, it covers the ceilings of almost all the rooms on the ground floor. There is also some exquisite oak carving in the window and door recesses by the master Vassily Zakharov. Fortunately it survived the war almost completely intact.

This room now contains exhibits introducing the visitor to the history of Alexandria and the Cottage.

Study of Alexandra Fyodorovna

The rooms facing west and north belonged to Nicholas I's wife, Alexandra, a Prussian princess. Next to her bedchamber was a small, but light Study with a bay window the upper section of which had stained glass in imitation of the stained glass in mediaeval castles. The furniture and most of the bronze and china items here are also in Gothic style or adorned with Gothic ornament. Many of them came to the Cottage in 1829. Of the sculptural works the marble bust of Nicholas I's daughter, Alexandra, by Ivan Vitaly and the bronze model of the gravestone for Queen Louisa of Prussia, Alexandra Fyodorovna's mother (1815, sculptor Christian Rauch), are worthy of note.

State Drawing Room

Menelaws planned this to be the main room on the ground floor. Note the stove and fireplace by the south wall that are adorned with carving, mirrors and marble. The superb moulding on the ceiling echoes the pattern of the large handwoven carpet covering the whole floor. The decor is completed by paintings and works of decorative and applied art.

Certain items are of special interest as, for example, the set of two candelabras and the clock in the form of the central portal of Rouen Cathedral, the work of Pyotr and Mikhail Vakhromeyev and Nikolai Yakovlev, masters of the Imperial Porcelain Works. Next to the clock on the mantelpiece are two identical Sevres vases presented by Napoleon I to the Russian Emperor Alexander I during their meeting at Tilsit.

In the middle of the room on a round table amid numerous caskets stands a silver Potsdam Cup with a rose on its top. The surface of the cup and the tray is decorated with enamelled coats-of-arms of German noble families. Three such cups were made by Berlin masters from a design by Karl Schinkel in 1830. Only this cup presented to Nicholas I has survived.

Among the pictures the works of Ivan Aivazovsky are of special interest. The Cottage has a whole collection of paintings by this fine master. There are four of his canvases in the Drawing Room: *View of Venice* (1842), two *Oriental Scenes* (1846) inspired by his visit to Turkey, and a *View of the Spit of Vassilievsky Island* (1847) showing the Bourse and Rostral Columns in the rays of the setting sun.

Library

The next room is the first of a suite of rooms used by all the inhabitants of the palace. The whole of the north wall is lined with Gothic bookcases, for which the room was specially designed. The other items are a desk, a screen with representations of ladies and knights in mediaeval dress, and a few chairs.

The Cottage Library contains more than 1,000 volumes, mainly works of fiction in German, English and French. The royal family were particularly fond of the novels of Sir Walter Scott. Pride of place in the Library is held by the multi-volume *Code of Laws of the Russian Empire* compiled in 1832 under the guidance of the Russian statesman Mikhail Speransky.

Note the painting hanging on the west wall by the staircase. It is *Tatiana Writing to Onegin* by Fyodor Moller, one of the first pictorial works on the subject of Pushkin's *Eugene Onegin*.

Cottage Palace   Marble terrace

Study of Alexandra Fyodorovna

Study of Nicholas I

Porcelain group from
Lesser Reception Hall

On the cabinet are sculptural portraits of Alexandra Fyodo-rovna's mother, Queen Louisa of Prussia, and her sister Frederica. These busts were made at the Berlin China Works in the 19th century from late 18th-century models by Johann Gottfried Scha-dow.

Of the other items in the room the clocks in the form of Gothic cathedrals and the model of a castle made of ivory and mother-of-pearl are of special interest.

Grand Reception Hall

One of the main features of the décor of this hall is the stove painted with Gothic ornament by Academician Giovanni Scotti. The walls are hung with pictures mainly by Russian painters: two views of Odessa (1829) by Maxim Vorobiev, *A View of Vesuvius in Winter* by Orest Kiprensky, *A View of Sorrento* (1826) by Sylvestr Shchedrin and others.

There is also a fine French silver chandelier in the shape of a basket of roses made in the late 1820s and a collection of Russian, French and German glass. But the china and glass in the next room, the Dining Hall, is particularly rich.

Dining Hall

The Dining Hall is divided into two sections by a vaulted arch on multi-faceted columns bearing the coat-of-arms of Alexandria. The smaller section is the old room; it was designed by Adam Mene-laws, while the larger one was built on by Andrei Stakenschneider in 1842.

In the middle of the hall is a huge leaf table with a white china dinner service made at the Imperial manufactory in St Petersburg specially for the Cottage. Each item is outlined delicately in gold and has the coat-of-arms of Alexandria emblazoned on it. Originally (in 1829) the service contained 314 pieces. It was later increased to 459 and continued to be added to right up to the beginning of the 20th century.

The service included 353 pieces of crystal, also decorated with the Alexandria coat-of-arms. This crystal, like the large crystal chandelier for 36 candles hanging above the table, was made at a glass factory in St Petersburg.

On the two shelves in the arcades are various items of glass by Italian, German, French and Russian masters.

Of the paintings the most interesting are three works by Théodore Gudin with panoramic views of the Alexandria Park from the balcony of the Cottage in the morning, afternoon and evening. Here too are works by Sokrat Vorobiev, Timofei Neff, Pimen Orlov and Ivan Aivazovsky.

Lesser Reception Hall

The walls here are painted to imitate wood. The numerous shelves have china figures and groups made in the middle of the 19th century at the Meissen porcelain works from 18th-century models. In the far corner from the window on a pedestal is a bronze bust of Alexandra Fyodorovna made by Pyotr Klodt from a model by the sculptor Christian Rauch. This bust used to stand in the summer-house to the south of the Cottage.

Staircase

All three floors of the palace are connected by the large wrought-iron staircase in the middle of the building. The wrought-iron balustrade with its light elegant Gothic design was manufactured at the Alexandrov works in St Petersburg. The staircase is lit by a lantern at the top. The sides of the staircase are painted by Giovanni Scotti in grisaille with Gothic pillars and arches receding into the distance. The pale blue background creates the impression of a deep blue sky.

On the lower landing tiled with marble is the bronze statue of
Glory by the sculptor Christian Rauch (1834-1841).

Rooms of the Heir to the Throne

The door from the first floor landing leads to a room with a semi-circular balcony. Passing this and the chamber which contains a bath carved out of a huge block of Carrara marble in the workshop of Paolo Triscorni, you come to the study room of the heir to the throne, the future Alexander II. The numerous paintings of military accoutrements, parades and changing of the guard and the tables illustrating military uniforms give a clear idea of the nature of his studies. The simple moulding round the edge of the ceiling in this room and the next, where the heir lived, is supplemented by grisaille painting in Gothic style.

Dressing Room

Behind the minute Valet's Room is Nicholas I's Dressing Room. The room's function is suggested by the huge marble-topped wash-stand, which, like the ash-wood cabinet, was made in the workshop of Heinrich Gambs. The china items in the room were made in St Petersburg. The coloured lithographs on the walls depict events in the Russo-Turkish War of 1828-1829.

The tambour in the corner conceals a spiral staircase down to the Library. It was through this apparently private room that the ministers passed to deliver their morning report to the Emperor in his study.

Study of Nicholas I

The ground plan of the Study is identical to that of the Grand Reception Hall below it, but its décor is far more austere. Instead of parquet the floor is covered with narrow planks in imitation of a ship's deck. There is no moulding on the ceiling. Instead a band of grisaille painting runs round the edge and moulded corbels along the top of the walls.

The furniture in the Study is also simple in form: two rectangular baize-topped desks, four cabinets, three divans of wavy birchwood, and some oak chairs. By the window is the camp-bed that followed Nicholas from palace to palace and was set up in his stady where he slept. It was on this bed that he died in the Winter Palace. The hard-backed chairs were made in 1840 on Nicholas' instructions from trees planted by Peter the Great in the Summer Garden that had been blown down by a storm.

On the cabinets and mantelpieces are busts of the Emperor's children, mostly the work of Karl Wichmann. The paintings are of particular value. By the windows are portrait miniatures by Louis Jean Lagrenée, Jean-Baptiste Isabey, Pyotr Sokolov, Christina Robertson and others. On the opposite wall are portraits of Alexander I and his wife Elizabeth by George Dawe and a portrait of Peter the Great on horseback by an unknown 18th-century painter.

Room of Maria Nikolayevna

The Emperor's rooms were followed by the chambers of his daughters. In the north-west corner was Maria's room. Later Nicholas II's mother, Maria Fyodorovna, lived in here, and the room was changed completely for her. It now contains a set of inlaid furniture made in the workshop of Andrei Tur in the middle of the 19th century. Most of the pictures, water colours and lithographs on the walls show Nicholas I at Peterhof.

By the north wall is an interesting clock with many dials showing the time in the sixty-six Russian provincial centres and also in Russian America, as Alaska was then called, which belonged to Russia until 1867. This clock was made in 1860 by Ivan Yurin and acquired by Alexander II. The Russian carpet was made in 1885.

In 1894 this room was decorated in Art Nouveau style from a design by Robert Melzer: the walls are hung with foliate-patterned printed fabric and the lower section is panelled with wood. All that remains of the original interior is the painted ceiling, the doors and windows and the marble fireplace made in the workshop of Paolo Triscorni. The furnishings are also in Art Nouveau style. The French porcelain vases and the figurines made by masters in the Danish Royal Manufactory in Copenhagen fit in well with the style of the room. There are also some late 19th-century Russian porcelain vases here.

Of the bronze articles the two splendid gilded figures of the dancer Loie Fuller cast in Paris from a model by Léonard van Weydeveldt deserve special attention. And of the paintings the works of Ivan Aivazovsky, Yuri Klever, Albert Benois, and Nikolai Prokofiev.

Room of Alexandra Nikolayevna

This is the only room belonging to a royal daughter that has survived in its original form. It belonged to Nicholas I's eldest daughter, Alexandra, who died at an early age. After her death the room was closed and all the things here were kept in memory of her.

The numerous knick-knacks, needlework items, and albums give one an idea of a typical young lady's room in a Russian home of the second quarter of the 19th century.

Marine Study

The rooms on the second floor did not have a set function. Sometimes they were used as nurseries and more often to accommodate members of the retinue and servants. Only one room facing the sea with a large balcony belonged to the Emperor. This was his private study. The splendid view of the Gulf and the town gave the room its name. The numerous instruments and other articles on the desk, such as a telescope, a compass, and a silver megaphone with the coat-of-arms of Alexandria, bear witness to the room's function.

On the walls are engravings of ships and harbours, and also lithographs depicting the defence of Sevastopol during the Crimean War (1853-1856).

On the right by the wall is a model of a monument to the Russian flotilla commander and Antarctic explorer Mikhail Lazarev (1788-1851).

From his Marine Study Nicholas I could observe the ships sailing from Kronstadt to St Petersburg and even supervise naval manoeuvres with the help of an optical telegraph. The tower from which he sent signals to Kronstadt was on the seashore opposite the Cottage.

* * *

You have now visited some of the palace museums and parks of Petrodvorets. This guide-book deals only with places that traditionally form part of the tourist's itinerary. But they are by no means all the sights of the town of Petrodvorets, the centre of a large Leningrad suburb that stretches for 37 kilometres along the southern shore of the Gulf of Finland and has a population of about 120,000. Apart from the ensembles described here there are the palaces and parks of the town of Lomonossov (former Oranienbaum), and those of Strelna.

In accordance with the master plan for Leningrad, this district is being developed as a public recreation zone and also a centre for scientific and cultural institutions. Construction is in progress on a university campus and some of the faculties of Leningrad University have already moved from Leningrad to Petrodvorets. A number of other higher educational establishments and scientific institutions are also being transferred here from Leningrad.

Petrodvorets also has a clock and watch factory. The Lapidary Works established in the reign of Peter the Great was turned into an industrial gems factory in Soviet times. In 1947 it began to manufacture clocks and watches. Today the Petrodvorets Clock and Watch Factory exports to more than twenty countries throughout the world.

The Petrodvorets Sanatorium next to the Lower Park makes use for medicinal purposes of mineral water supplied by a spring in its own grounds.

The palaces and parks continue to play an important part in the life of the district. Each year new rooms, even whole palaces, that have been resurrected thanks to the efforts of restorers are opened to the public. As well as the five museums open at present restoration work is being carried out on the Farm Palace and Capella in the Alexandria Park, the Catherine Palace and Bathing Pools in Monplaisir, the Assembly Hall, and the Kitchen. It is planned to restore the interiors of the East Wing and Coat-of-Arms Pavilion of the Great Palace. The Tsarina's Pavilion on the pond to the south of the Upper Park is also in process of restoration. The work being carried out in the Lower Park is extensive and costly. It is aimed at restoring this fine specimen of park architecture to its original form of an 18th-century formal park.

The palace museums of Petrodvorets maintain contacts with many large museums throughout the world. The links with the Sans Souci palace complex in Potsdam (GDR) with which Petrodvorets has an agreement on cooperation are particularly fruitful.

Its proximity to Leningrad, good communications and the many and varied impressions that Petrodvorets offers visitors have made it the most popular tourist attraction in the Soviet Union.

Information

By train from Baltiisky Station to Novy Petergof
Station (thirty to forty minutes) and then by bus.
By *Meteor* motorboat (May to September) from the
Hermitage, Ploschad Dekabristov and Tuchkov
Bridge landing-stages in Leningrad to the Lower
Park (twenty-five minutes).

The fountains in the Lower Park and Upper
Gardens play from May to September daily from
11 a.m. to 6 p.m.

Great Palace. Open daily (Mondays excepted)
from 11 a.m. to 6 p.m. Closed on the last Tuesday
of each month.
Monplaisir. Open daily from May to September
(Wednesdays excepted) from 11 a.m. to 6 p.m.
Closed on the last Thursday of each month.
Hermitage. Open daily from May to September
(Wednesdays excepted) from 11 a. m. to 6 p. m.
Closed on the last Thursday of each month.
Château de Marly. Open daily (Tuesdays excepted)
from 11 a.m. to 6 p.m. Closed on the last Wednesday
of each month.

Cottage. Open daily, (except Monday in winter
and Friday in summer) from 11 a.m. to 6 p.m.
Closed on the last Tuesday of each month in winter
and the last Thursday of each month in summer.

Each year on a Sunday in August the traditional
Festival of Fountains is held to commemorate the
first time that the Peterhof fountains began to
play. During the White Nights Festival of Arts in
Leningrad there is also a festival at Peterhof. In the
summer season various festivals and celebrations
are held almost every Sunday.

INTOURIST—11 Isaakiyevskaya Ploshchad
SPUTNIK—4 Ulitsa Chapygina
VNESHTORGBANK—2 Ulitsa Brodskogo
INGOSSTRAKH—17 Ulitsa Kalyayeva
SOCIETY FOR FRIENDSHIP AND CULTURAL
RELATIONS (Leningrad branch)—21
Naberezhnaya reki Fontanki

ASTORIA—39 Ulitsa Herzena (Metro—*Nevsky
Prospekt*)
YEVROPEISKAYA—1/7 Ulitsa Brodskogo
(Metro—*Nevsky Prospekt*)
KARELIA—27/2 Ulitsa Tukhachevskogo
LENINGRAD—5/2 Pirogovskaya Naberezhnaya
(Metro—*Ploshchad Lenina*),

PRIBALTIISKAYA—14 Ulitsa Korablestroitelei, Harbour district (Metro—*Primorskaya*)

A Bureau de Change can be found at the airport, the seaport and the Astoria, Yevropeiskaya, Karelia, Leningrad and Pribaltiiskaya hotels. Opening hours are 9 a.m. to 2 p.m. and 3 p.m. to 8 p.m. daily. Unused Soviet currency may be changed back at the airport or seaport.

Postcards, stamps and envelopes are on sale at stationary kiosks and post offices. Blue post-boxes are for out of town mail and abroad, and red post-boxes for local mail only.
Registered letters, small parcels and telegrams may be sent from hotel post offices or any other post office in the city.
Leningrad Central Post Office—9 Ulitsa Soyuza Svyazi
Leningrad Central Telegraph—14 Ulitsa Soyuza Svyazi
Parcels abroad can be sent from the Central Post Office (open from 9 a.m. to 9 p.m., Sundays from 10 a.m. to 8 p.m.).
All mail and telegrams are also handled here. Foreign languages spoken.
If you do not know at what hotel you will be staying we would advise you to give your correspondents the following address: Leningrad.

Central Post Office, Poste Restante, and your name.

Letters will be kept for you for 30 days and telegrams for 45 days.

In the Soviet Union certain items may not be sent out of the country by post. These include jewelry, amber, antiques, films and postage stamps (used and unused). If you have any queries regarding items to be sent by post you should consult the staff of the Central Post Office.

Postal and telegraphic charges in respect of other countries may vary in accordance with international agreements between the country in question and the USSR.

Telephone calls to other cities in the Soviet Union and abroad may be ordered at the service bureau in your hotel and taken in your room. They can also be ordered at special telephone exchanges. A list of these is available from your hotel service bureau.

Type	Hours	Fares (single journey)	Charges per item of hand luggage (exceeding 30 kg in weight and 60×40×20 cm in size)
Bus	6 a. m. to 1 a. m.	5 kopecks	10 kopecks
Trolley-bus	6 a. m. to to 1 a. m.	5 kopecks	10 kopecks
Tram	5.30 a. m. to 1 a. m.	5 kopecks	10 kopecks
Metro	5.35 a. m. to 1 a. m.	5 kopecks	two five-ko-peck pieces
Taxi-bus		15 копecks	
Taxi	24 hours	20 kopecks per km plus 20 kopecks initial charge (irrespective of number of passengers)	no charge

Children under seven travel free on all forms of transport.

There are no conductors on buses, trolleybuses and trams. Tickets are obtained for these forms of transport by putting the correct fare into the box provided and tearing off the requisite number of tickets. The fare covers the cost of a single journey from one terminus to the other. Tickets must be retained until the end of the journey.

On taxi-buses the driver collects the fare.
In the entrance halls of the metro there are machines
that give change for 20, 15 and 10 kopeck pieces in
five-kopeck pieces. The fare covers journeys in any
direction and any number of changes.
In buses, trolleybuses and trams you can buy books
of tickets from the driver (10 tickets per book).
These tickets are then punched on special machines
which are usually near the ticket boxes.
It is best to order a taxi in advance through your
service bureau or find one at a taxi rank. The cost
of the journey is indicated on the meter.

For Motorists

Driving in the USSR is on the right.
It is strictly prohibited to drink and drive.
In urban areas horns may be sounded only to avoid
an accident.
Road signs in the USSR are international.
The speed limit in built-up areas is 60 kph (38 mph)
unless otherwise indicated. In rural areas it is
80 kmph (50 mph) unless otherwise indicated.
Parking is free and permitted anywhere unless there
is a public transport stop or a prohibitive sign. There
are also special parking lots with a charge of
30 kopecks a day per car and 50 kopecks a day
per coach.

INDEX

CASCADES AND FONTAINS

For notes

Редактор русского текста *Я. Бродский*
Контрольный редактор *А. Кафыров*
Художник *В. Мирошниченко*
Художественный редактор *А. Томчинская*
Технический редактор *С. Сизова*

ИБ № 1559

Сдано в набор 26.09.85. Подписано в печать
03.06.86. Формат 70×100^1/$_{32}$. Бумага мелованная.
Гарнитура таймс. Печать офсетная. Условн. печ. л.
7,1. Усл. кр.-отт. 40,8. Уч.-изд. л. 9,79. Тираж
82 920 экз. Заказ № 2437. Цена 2 руб. Изд. № 1815

Издательство «Радуга» Государственного
комитета СССР по делам издательств, полиграфии
и книжной торговли.
Москва, 119859, Зубовский бульвар, 17

Ордена Трудового Красного Знамени Калининский
полиграфический комбинат Союзполиграфпрома
при Государственном комитете СССР по делам
издательств, полиграфии и книжной торговли.
170024, г. Калинин, пр. Ленина, 5.